The Librarian's Guide to

INTELLECTUAL PROPERTY

in the Digital Age

Copyrights, Patents, and Trademarks

Timothy Lee Wherry

American Library Association
Chicago and London
2002

The paper used in this publication meets the minimum requirements of American National Standard for Information Sciences—Permanence of Paper for Printed Library Materials, ANSI Z39.48-1992. ∞

Composition by ALA Editions in Franklin Gothic and Janson Text using QuarkXPress 4.14 for the PC. Printed on 50-pound white offset and bound in 10-point coated cover stock by McNaughton & Gunn.

ISBN: 8389-0825-X

Printed in the United States of America

06   05   04   03   02   5   4   3   2   1

For Will, Asa, and Lori

Contents

Introduction

Writing and speaking about intellectual property over the past twenty years have shown me that most people are interested in patents, copyright, and trademarks but do not know where to find concise, useful information. Usually the interest in intellectual property begins with a product that a person has invented or a design or image that he or she wishes to copyright or trademark. If they persevere, people will seek assistance with this very complicated procedure, and the contact person is often a librarian or a teacher.

Librarians at large, metropolitan public libraries receive requests for patent information daily. Educators at colleges and universities have to field a variety of questions dealing with intellectual property, especially as it relates to information on the Internet. With the advent of the Internet, concerns about legally downloading images, music, and text are ongoing for both librarians and educators. The principal problem is that most intellectual property questions do not have simple answers. The systems that govern patents, copyrights, and trademarks are very confusing and complicated even for those who work with them all the time.

The majority of books and websites on the topic are written by legal professionals who direct their messages to other professionals or to those who already possess a basic knowledge of intellectual property. Even recent books and websites begin with the assumption that the reader already knows something about copyright. These resources take the reader on a journey through intellectual property that can be understood only with the aid of a specially trained librarian or professor. They present technical explanations and detailed demonstrations of forms, laws, and esoteric information for which a novice has no need.

People are fascinated by intellectual property, but frustrated in finding some way to obtain sufficient information quickly and at their level. It was from that basic premise that I decided to write this book. It is my intention that readers enjoy this book and, more importantly, gain an adequate knowledge of patents, copyrights, and trademarks in the digital age so they can make informed decisions about their creative efforts.

This book will not make the reader an expert, but it does provide enough information to understand the system without a great deal of confusion and toil. It will give educators and librarians enough information to be able to converse with students and library users effectively.

Although the process of writing a book is undertaken by a single individual, there is more to it than merely typing the words. This book is the product of the efforts of many people. I would like to thank Kevin Harwell, another Penn State librarian, for knowing more than I do about patents and always being able to answer any question I asked him. Jim Hutchens, a former Penn State librarian, prepared the first bibliography that gave me the foundation to proceed with the manuscript. Dr. Bob Hendrickson, associate dean for Graduate Studies and Research at Penn State, first suggested to me that I attempt to write something on intellectual property in the digital age. Jack Sulzer, associate dean for Commonwealth Campus Libraries, provided the staffing and support that allowed me to take sabbatical to prepare the manuscript. Mary Hooper, staff assistant at Robert E. Eiche Library, helped with typing, located websites, prepared illustrations, proofread each chapter, and handled the hundred details that go into actually putting a book together. And, finally, thanks to my muse, Katie Scarlet.

Chapter 1

An Introduction to Intellectual Property: Copyrights, Patents, and Trademarks

All intellectual property protection in the United States is granted by Article 1, Section 8 of the Constitution: "Congress shall have the power . . . to promote the progress of science and useful arts, by securing for limited times to authors and inventors the exclusive rights to their respective writings and discoveries." Virtually every publication dealing with intellectual property mentions this for an important reason. The U.S. Constitution was the first modern constitution to convey these rights as a basic principle of government. The framers of the Constitution realized that the concept of profiting from the fruits of one's intellect would motivate creative people and, ultimately, add to the wealth of the new country. Obviously they were right. It has been estimated that 80 percent of the wealth of the United States comes directly or indirectly from intellectual property.

Volumes of law books and hundreds of court cases are the result of these few lines of the Constitution. The biggest obstacle to the application of intellectual property law to various situations in recent years has been the impact of technology on laws that were not designed with technology in mind. For example, photography fit very nicely into the existing concepts of copyright law because it was just another means of painting or drawing; motion pictures, however, did not. In the early days of film, each frame of motion picture film was copyrighted separately, because the Copyright Office (a branch of the Library of Congress) didn't quite know how to treat it. A recurring theme of intellectual property, and especially patents, is that new technologies are forced into existing categories. This is often seen in the way new technologies are named. The automobile was first called a "horseless carriage," but it wasn't really a carriage that didn't have a horse. Rockets that travel out of earth's orbit are called space "ships." The radio was first called a "wireless." In 1942 when the first photocopy machine was patented, the patent examiners didn't know what to do with it. The title of the patent is "electrophotography." It was something completely new.

The concept of intellectual property law's not keeping pace with technology is not a new one. But it is clear that as technology advances more quickly, the law often lags so far behind that its relevance creates more than minor dilemmas. It is also clear that the traditional tools used in intellectual property research—patent searching tools, for example—are not the first business tools to enjoy the benefits of new technologies.

Before proceeding with an explanation of how intellectual property is affected by technology, any treatment of patents, copyrights, and trademarks must begin with an understanding of the terms and concepts that relate to these three major types of intellectual property. The primary confusion in the minds of many library users relates to what types of protection apply to a given thing. Even lawyers can get confused about the extent of intellectual property protection provided by a patent as opposed to, say, a copyright. It's not unusual to hear that someone is in the process of "patenting a name" or "copyrighting a slogan." Some manufacturers and inventors deliberately use this confusion to their advantage. For example, the Trivial Pursuit board game carries a copyright symbol on its box. This does not mean that the game is copyrighted. The artwork on the box is copyrighted. The game itself is patented.

On a basic level, patents concern functional things, copyrights concern artistic works, and trademarks protect the word or symbol that identifies a given product in the mind of the consumer. When it is said that patents protect *functional* things, it means that the physical thing or process being patented must have a practical use. The patented item does not have to be a physical thing, however; patents can be granted on a process of manufacturing goods or carrying out business. This particular area has caused controversy. For example, in 1997, amazon.com was granted a patent on its "one click" method of ordering books online. This method allowed customers who had previously registered with amazon.com to click on a single button to order an item. This was a new process for Amazon, but not exactly an innovative or unheard-of concept in online merchandising. Because amazon.com had patented the process, however, other online retailers, such as

Barnes and Noble, couldn't use the method. In a suit brought by Barnes and Noble, a federal judge ruled that Barnes and Noble could use a "two click" method of ordering. This was an issue that the framers of the Constitution had never foreseen. The rule that a thing or process must be new and unique will be discussed in the chapters on patents later in this book.

COPYRIGHT

Copyright concerns artistic expression. The major point here is that, unlike for a patent, the thing being copyrighted must be functionless or useless. Copyright is protection for the expression of an artistic idea that is "fixed in some tangible means," according to Title 17 of the U.S. Code. That is, the artistic expression is written on paper or painted on canvas or recorded on tape. The idea in the artist's or author's mind must take a physical form. A person could copyright a book but couldn't patent a book because a book has no function.

An exercise often used in classrooms and seminars demonstrates how important it is to "fix" an idea in some tangible form. In this exercise, the participants form small groups of three or four. Each group comes up with an idea for a sculpture, a painting, or a gizmo of some sort. On a piece of paper, each group explains its idea in writing. On a second sheet of paper, the group actually draws the thing they have in mind. Each group then exchanges the written part of the exercise with another group. This new group then tries to draw the sculpture or gizmo using only the written explanation. When these drawings are shared with the entire group, the thing that became "fixed" is usually nothing like the original drawing by the group that first "invented" the item. This demonstrates how important it is for an artist to protect her physical version of what she has imagined and how that "fixed" creation is unique to the person who imagined. More detailed information on what types of items can and cannot be copyrighted can be found in the chapters on copyright later in this book.

PATENTS

Patents are divided into three types: utility patents (which also have three types: mechanical, electrical, and chemical), design patents, and plant patents. Utility patents cover those things we normally think of as inventions—a toilet paper holder that is also a radio, or a photocopy machine, or a perpetual motion machine (no, there has never been a patent granted on a perpetual motion machine).

Design patents are granted on the design of a functional thing. This is cause for much misunderstanding because protection of artistic or design items is normally provided by copyright. A sculpture or a photograph, for example, is protected by copyright, not by a patent. The distinction involves function: a design patent is granted on an item that serves a function, like a door knob shaped like a sculpture; copyright is granted on items that are purely artistic. For example, the buckle on a belt would be protected by a design patent rather than a copyright. A belt buckle has a particular function and the designer of the buckle is not reinventing the belt buckle itself (which would be protected by a utility patent), but only changing its design. A book would be protected by copyright because, in patent terminology, a book is useless. That is, it serves no *functional* purpose.

One unusual design patent has been granted on a water closet on a toilet that also serves as an aquarium (see fig. 1.1). Again, the water tank is not being invented; only its design is changed. (Those wondering what happens to the fish when the toilet is flushed will be relieved to know that the aquarium is an insert within the tank and the water in it does not flush.) Another example of a design patent is a doorstop that is shaped like a book. If this object were a book itself, it would be protected by a copyright, but because it serves a function, it is protected by a design patent.

A plant patent is granted on a new type of plant that is created by human intervention and is produced asexually. A person who finds a new kind of plant growing wild in a field could not patent that plant, but a person who can show that he or she has taken cuttings and manipulated generations of several plants to create a new plant could patent the new plant. Many people have heard of "patent roses." Such roses are created by horticultural manipulation and are not naturally occurring plants.

TRADEMARKS

Trademarks concern the identification of commercial origin. Trademarks protect "any word, name, symbol, or device, or any combination thereof adopted by a manufacturer or merchant to identify his goods and distinguish them from those manufactured or sold by others." The current law, the Lanham Act (P. L. 489), was enacted in 1946.

Trademarks are granted in five categories. A trademark may be a brand name, trade dress, service mark, certification mark, or collective mark. For

FIGURE 1.1

Toilet Tank with Aquarium

United States Patent [19]

Everson

[11] **Des. 270,936**

[45] ** **Oct. 11, 1983**

[54] **COMBINED TOILET TANK AND AQUARIUM**

[76] Inventor: D. Randall Everson, 18615 Loree Ave., Cupertino, Calif. 95014

[**] Term: **14 Years**

[21] Appl. No.: 227,164

[22] Filed: **Jan. 22, 1981**

[51] Int. Cl. .... **D23—02**
[52] U.S. Cl. **D23/49; D23/66; D30/11**

[58] Field of Search D23/49, 65–67; D30/11; 4/353, 661; 119/5

[56] **References Cited**

U.S. PATENT DOCUMENTS

D. 101,441	10/1936	Dreyfuss	D23/65
D. 179,484	1/1957	Lampkins	D30/11
D. 199,729	12/1964	Kaiser	D23/66
D. 229,766	1/1971	Kephart	D30/11
830,286	9/1906	Alexander	D23/66 X
918,456	4/1909	Marcellus	D23/66 X

2,238,699	4/1941	Levine	4/353
3,968,525	7/1976	Alexander	D23/66 X
4,364,132	12/1982	Robinson	4/661 X

Primary Examiner—James R. Largen
Attorney, Agent, or Firm—Thomas E. Schatzel

[57] **CLAIM**

The ornamental design for a combined toilet tank and aquarium, as shown and described.

DESCRIPTION

FIG. 1 is a perspective view taken from the top, front and left side of a combined toilet tank and aquarium showing my new design;
FIG. 2 is a front elevational view thereof;
FIG. 3 is a top plan view thereof;
FIG. 4 is a bottom plan view thereof;
FIG. 5 is a left side elevational view thereof;
FIG. 6 is a right side elevational view thereof; and
FIG. 7 is a rear elevational view thereof.
The broken line representation of plants and gravel in FIGS. 1 and 2, a toilet bowl in FIG. 1 and plumbing hardware in FIG. 7 is for purposes of illustration only and form no part of the claimed design.

example, the name Sara Lee on baked goods is a brand name; the shape of the Coca-Cola bottle is trade dress (and is also covered by a design patent because it is a functional item); the little red-haired girl that identifies all Wendy's restaurants is a service mark; the joined red, yellow, and blue diamonds that identify American steel or the Pittsburgh Steelers football team constitute a certification mark; and the multicolored NASCAR automobile racing logo that identifies goods, services, and races sponsored and certified by NASCAR is a collective mark.

Good examples of well-known trademarks are the golden arches of McDonald's or Wendy's "Where's the Beef?" slogan. Yes, that slogan is a trademark and not a copyright, even though it is a phrase that serves no function. Phrases, like those seen on bumper stickers or T-shirts, are not eligible for copyright protection (see the chapters on copyright). "Where's the Beef?" is protected by a trademark as an identifying phrase of Wendy's restaurants.

It has been reported that the most recognizable trademark in the world is the Coca-Cola logo, supposedly recognized even by people in primitive regions. A close second would be the golden arches of McDonald's.

EXAMPLES OF INTELLECTUAL PROPERTY

Traditionally, trademark protection was granted *after* a mark or phrase appeared on a product or service. With patents and copyright, the protection is granted *before* the item is used or displayed in public or *at the moment* of its being "fixed in a tangible form." The easiest way to define how protection applies to each type of intellectual property is by examining three examples—a table lamp, a console television, and the Rolls-Royce hood ornament.

Think of a table lamp with an ornamental base. The base is sculpted of molded metal in the shape of a tree trunk. The shade is stained glass with a leaf pattern. A patent would protect the elements of the lamp that are functional, such as the wired base that looks like a tree trunk. This would be a *design* patent because the lamp itself is not being invented. Only the *shape* of its base is unique. A copyright would protect the shade as a piece of artwork if it stood alone. The shade serves a functional purpose and could also be protected by a design patent. A trademark would protect the brand name for the lamp.

A console television would be protected by patent on all the components of the television that are functional—the electronics of the television that are new and unobvious. A design patent would protect the ornamental aspects of the cabinet. A trademark would protect the brand name of the television. Copyright would protect the artistic elements of the cabinet that are not functional and are purely decorative. And, of course, copyright would protect the programs viewed on the television.

Charles Sykes, a famous sculptor of the time, created the Rolls-Royce automobile hood ornament, known as the "Flying Lady," in 1910. Sykes named the sculpture "The Spirit of Ecstasy," allegedly after riding in a Silver Ghost Rolls-Royce. The Flying Lady is protected by a copyright because it was, in its inception, a sculpture. The Flying Lady is also the registered trademark of the Rolls-Royce automobile company. But how is the Flying Lady protected by a patent, since it seems to be a purely decorative and nonfunctional piece of art? Originally, the sculpture functioned as the automobile's radiator cap. In this capacity, it was protected by a design patent—a design that appears on a functional item.

Now that the basics of intellectual property are a bit clearer, it is useful to wade a bit deeper into the intellectual property waters and see why technology brings a new set of problems to the issue. All intellectual property protection, especially copyright, has been confusing since the United States first granted it. The purpose of this book is to clear up some of the confusion surrounding intellectual property protection, especially as it relates to electronic media.

Chapter 2

Copyright

According to Title 17 of the United States Code, "Copyright must be an original work of authorship fixed in a tangible medium of expression." Copyright grants to its holder certain exclusive rights of use and control as long as the thing being copyrighted is "fixed."

If a woman gives an impromptu speech before a group, she cannot copyright it. If a person does a little dance on impulse, the dance cannot be copyrighted. An improvised speech or a spontaneous jig cannot be copyrighted because they are not fixed in a medium of expression. However, if the speech is recorded or written down as it is given, it now becomes *fixed* in a tangible medium and can be protected by copyright. If the dance is written as steps of choreography or if it is videotaped, those tangible forms of expression can be copyrighted.

Once an artistic expression takes a tangible form, the copyright holder has five exclusive rights: the right to copy; the right to prepare derivative works; the right to distribute copies; the right to perform the work publicly; and the right to display the work publicly. (Although these last two rights seem to be similar, the right to display a work is a very important concept in the field of distance education. More about that later.) Although the five rights are explained later in this chapter, it is easier to explain first what *cannot* be copyrighted because these points are more specific than those for what *can* be copyrighted.

WHAT CANNOT BE COPYRIGHTED

The most important guide to what cannot be copyrighted is that all copyrighted things must be *fixed* in some medium of expression. They must be written, recorded, photographed, painted, drawn, or shaped in some material. Anything that does not exist in some physical medium cannot be copyrighted.

That being said, there are things that, even if they are expressed through a physical medium, cannot be copyrighted. Slogans cannot be copyrighted. This is always a shock to those who dream of great riches from creating a slogan for a bumper sticker or a T-shirt. The first question from those who are informed that slogans cannot be copyrighted is "What about 'The Joy of Cola' or 'Where's the Beef?' or 'You Deserve a Break Today'?" The answer is that these slogans are company trademarks and are not copyrighted. A person who did not create the slogan cannot use it for his or her own purposes, not because it's copyrighted, but because it's a trademark.

Familiar symbols or designs cannot be copyrighted. One example is the star pattern of the Big Dipper. Another example is the American flag. The premise behind this rule is that if something is already familiar to millions, one person cannot claim exclusive rights to it. Imagine the problem if any time somebody wanted to use the Big Dipper in star charts and the like, he or she would have to get permission from the owner of the Big Dipper star pattern.

Listings of ingredients are not copyrightable. The most obvious reason is that there is nothing artistic or creative about listing things. Also, the negative implication of copyrighting lists of ingredients (for example, flour, baking soda, and salt) is that nobody else could use that same list even if his or her product contained exactly the same things. The natural extension is not allowing protection on a very common list—the phone book. After all, the phone book is a simple listing of public information. It is not presented in a unique or artistic way, and most phone books are very similar in format. Copyrights have been granted on unique phone books, however—phone books that do uncommon things. For example, certain city directories numerically list phone numbers. That is, you can look up a phone number to find a person's name. Very handy if you have a number written on a piece of paper and don't know to whom it belongs. That type of listing is unique and unusual and, therefore, copyrightable.

Common-property works are not copyrightable. An example of a common-property work is a height-and-weight chart. These charts are distributed by insurance companies or health organizations and are based on statistical information. They are all the same in giving an indication of what range of weight is common for various heights, and none can claim to be the tangible result of a person's artistic inspiration.

For the same reasons, standard calendars are not copyrightable. Every calendar has the same information, such as May 9, 2001, is a Wednesday or June 2001 has five Saturdays. But during Christmas season in every mall, there is a calendar store with hundreds of varieties of calendars, each bearing a copyright symbol. Just as the copyright symbol on the Trivial Pursuit game is for the box artwork and not the game itself, the copyright symbol on calendars is for their artwork or other artistic expression, not for the information they present. The copyright on a calendar showing houses designed by Frank Lloyd Wright is for the photos or drawings of the houses. A calendar with twelve pictures of cats has a copyright on those pictures but not on the calendar itself.

Ideas and methods are not copyrightable because they usually are not fixed in a medium. If the idea were drawn or the methods explained in text, copyright could be granted on the drawing or the instructions, but not on the idea or method itself. Someone could steal the idea or method, but not make copies of the instructions. However, ideas and methods are patentable (see fig. 2.1 and the chapters on patenting). It should be clear that even trying to explain minor aspects of copyright law is very difficult. Murky or confusing application of the law is a hallmark of copyright and this problem will become more evident as more characteristics of copyright are explained.

RIGHTS OF THE COPYRIGHT HOLDER

Every copyright holder is granted five exclusive rights.

The Right to Copy

The right to copy is one of the few clearer concepts of copyright law. If one creates something artistic that is fixed in some medium, only that person who created the work (or holds the copyright) may make a copy of the thing created. The most well-known artistic creation in the area of copyright is a book. If an author writes a book (it need not be published), only the author can make a copy of all or part of the book. It is this most clearly understood concept that was the basis for an important legal concept dealing with technology. That is, is the Xerox® machine legal since its purpose is to allow others to make copies? It is, because in addition to the ability to make illegal copies, a photocopy machine can also make legal copies.

FIGURE 2.1
Patent Illustration

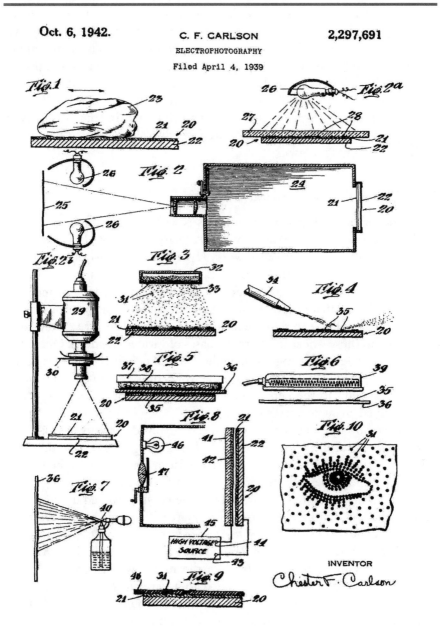

Oct. 6, 1942.   C. F. CARLSON   2,297,691
ELECTROPHOTOGRAPHY
Filed April 4, 1939

INVENTOR
Chester F. Carlson

Suppose a person purchases an original oil painting. The artist who created the work holds the copyright on that painting, but because it has been purchased and is the only one of its kind, who holds the right to make copies of the painting? The artist. Even though a person pays good money to own a work of art, the copyright rights remain with the artist. This is an important concept for museums that purchase works of art at very great prices. Such purchase does not give the museum the right to copy a painting. Even if a person has an original work of art in her home that she legally purchased, she may not make copies of that work of art. In some cases, even photographs of the painting, if they are later displayed publicly, may be in violation of copyright law.

The Right to Prepare Derivative Works

The best way to explain derivative works is with some examples: A movie made from a book is a derivative work. A board game based on a popular television program is a derivative work. A play, like the musical *Cats*, which is based on a concept devised by T. S. Eliot, is a derivative work.

This last type of derivative work—a concept that is fixed in one medium of expression and that originated in another medium—often is misused and misunderstood. The entertainment industry is careful to give credit—and payment—to those whose ideas are the bases of various creations. Often, the credits for a television program include a line like "Characters created by John Smith" or "Characters based on the works of John Smith." This statement gives credit to the person who created the personalities from which the portrayed characters were drawn.

A few years ago, a high-profile legal case involved derivative works. The actor Eddie Murphy made a movie titled *Coming to America* that was released in 1988. The plot concerns a rich African who arrives in the United States and experiences culture shock. The movie was successful and grossed over $140 million before a suit was filed. The lawsuit claimed that the concept for the plot originated from another source. The famous columnist Art Buchwald contended that *Coming to America* was based on a two-page treatment that Buchwald had sold to Paramount Pictures in 1983 titled *King for a Day*. Buchwald claimed that because the movie was a derivative work based on his treatment, he was entitled to a percentage of the film's net profit. In the historic lawsuit that followed, Paramount contended that the film had actually made no profit, so there was no reason to pay Buchwald. Of course, the successful film had earned millions, but in the byzantine methods of Hollywood studio accounting, no profit was shown. When the suit was settled, "Hollywood math" was changed forever. Art Buchwald's settlement came to more than $1 million. Not bad for a two-page plot summary. The important point here is that the source of a derivative work is protected intellectual property, no matter how small.

The Right to Distribute Copies

The right to distribute copies belongs to the copyright holder even if "distributing copies" is interpreted as handing out photocopies in a classroom. (See chapter 3 on fair use for legal ways to hand out copied materials in an educational setting.) In the digital world, distributing copies also means posting material on a website because in reality this is distribution worldwide.

For librarians, an important issue was addressed in the case of *Hotaling v. Church of Jesus Christ of Latter-day Saints*. Under certain conditions, a library is considered to be distributing materials when it circulates a book. Normally, this is an educational, not-for-profit "fair use"; however, in certain cases when protected materials have been put into a library collection, the library may be in violation of copyright law. For example, a member of the Church of Jesus Christ of Latter-day Saints buys materials from her church that are intended to be used by church members only. After deciding not to follow Mormon principles, she donates the materials to a library. The library accepts them and adds them to the circulating collection, unaware that the materials are intended for use by church members only. When these materials are circulated, the library is in violation of the right of distribution, which belongs to the copyright holder only.

In the digital world, there is a court case that is very similar to the preceding scenario. In the case of *Religious Technology Center v. Netcom*, materials owned by the Church of Scientology were placed on an Internet newsgroup through a server controlled by Netcom. The church wanted the materials removed because they were proprietary to the church and not for public distribution. Netcom refused to do this. The court found that neither Netcom nor the newsgroup that posted the material had been guilty of direct infringement on the copyright because neither party took action to make copies. Unfortunately, the parties settled out of court and the materials were removed without monetary damages being awarded to the church. It is important to note here that this action took place in 1995, three years before the Digital Millennium Copyright Act gave immunity to Internet service providers if they were unaware of illegal practices by their customers and before there was a clear understanding as to whether posting material on the Internet is, in reality, distribution.

Those who have been in high school or community theatre productions may have wondered why each cast member got only one copy of the script, and, after the performance, had to return the script. It is because of copyright. Each play booklet is a copyrighted copy of an author's work. By giving each cast member a script, the theatre is distributing the script. The playwright is entitled to royalties from and control of such distribution. The playwright will allow it, for a fee, but all copies have to be returned to the playwright or her agents. The playwright will also allow it because the play's public performance will produce more royalties.

The Right to Perform a Work Publicly

When a play is performed for an audience, it is publicly performed. This right belongs to a copyright holder. If he allows the play to be performed by others, he is entitled to a royalty fee and control over how the work is performed. This is a pretty straightforward concept, but it gets muddied when a work is performed in an educational setting.

For example, reading from textbooks or novels would be permitted in a classroom setting, as would singing a popular tune. However, stage plays cannot be performed in a classroom nor can a student perform a song from an opera. The difference is that the first type of performance involves non-dramatic works while the second type, which is prohibited, includes dramatic works that are intended to be performed.

In distance education, even more problems arise. In a classroom, an instructor may play a videotape or DVD, play a slide show, or play a multimedia program without authorization from the author under the guidelines of fair use. But, in distance education, none of these activities is considered legal (see chapter 3 on fair use for more examples of limits on distance education). By being transmitted over a television or satellite or the Web, the work is in essence being "performed publicly" and is not limited to an educational environment. In some cases, the law permits performances in distance education if the delivery site is a place where people gather for educational purposes, such as a high school classroom or an auditorium. But in distance education, the program might also be delivered into somebody's living room. The law is unclear as to whether this would qualify as a place specifically for educational purposes.

A common question about performing works publicly concerns music played by radio stations. The music is free and the royalties for one song being played once must be minuscule, so how would an artist control these performances and collect royalties? The answer is that radio stations make a note of every song played and pay a royalty every so often to license these songs. That fee and record of what was played go to an agency that collects fees and distributes them to the artists or their representatives.

The Right to Display a Work Publicly

Previously, we had an example of a person owning a painting created by another person. It is assumed that when a painting is sold, it will be displayed in a person's home, and an exemption in copyright law allows purchasers of such art to display it. But if the owner of the painting displays the work at an art show, this may be a violation of copyright, because the creator of the painting holds display rights even though she no longer owns the painting. The same rights of a purchaser to display a work of art do not apply to works *performed* publicly, however.

In an educational setting, it may be fair use for an instructor to display a copy of a painting in an art class, but such fair use disappears if the course is a distance-learning course. In a distance-learning course, the painting may be placed on a website that is accessible to everybody in the world, making it a public display and not exclusively an educational display in a classroom.

HOW LONG DOES A COPYRIGHT LAST?

Copyright lasts the life of the author plus seventy years after his or her death. The current copyright law originally gave an author rights for a lifetime plus fifty years, but that law was amended by the Sonny Bono (yes, *that* Sonny Bono) Term Extension Act (1998), which Bono sponsored when he was a congressman from California. The purpose of the extension was to protect certain artists of the rock and roll era who died young and whose copyrights could expire while the music was still popular. Without the extension, the music of artists like Buddy Holly, who died in the 1950s, and Janis Joplin, who died in the 1960s, could enter the public domain in the next few years.

For an anonymous work, copyright lasts 95 years from the date of registration or 125 years from the date of creation, whichever is shorter. Note that since 1988, it is not required that a work of art be registered in order to claim copyright. Copyright is assumed on creation. Even those crayon drawings that your mother put on the refrigerator are copyrighted works of art. It is also not necessary to display the copyright symbol (©) on works. But if a copyright is not registered with the Library of Congress, the burden of proof of ownership of the copyright rests with the copyright holder.

Chapter 3

Fair Use

Within the current copyright law is a codified concept called "fair use" (Section 107). Fair use is a loophole in the copyright law that allows someone other than the copyright holder to copy and distribute copyrighted material under certain conditions without first obtaining permission. It has been said that fair use is the safety valve of copyright because without it, copyright's constitutional purpose to promote learning, advance knowledge, and promote the progress of science would be useless. The law specifically allows fair use for such purposes as criticism, comment, news reporting, teaching, and scholarship or research. That being said, trying to decipher those purposes and conditions is a daunting and confusing task.

Fair use is the most important concept relating to intellectual property that educators and librarians are likely to face. Fair use is a significant issue for educators in that it is used daily in instruction but it is not clearly defined. Although fair use has been claimed for two hundred years in the United States, it has been spelled out in the law only since 1978. Before 1978, fair use evolved through a series of court decisions into a slippery and vague concept.

Fair use evolved as courts tried to balance the rights of copyright holders and society's interest in making copies of a work, primarily for teaching and news reporting. If not for fair use, every time a librarian or teacher wanted to use copyrighted material for educational purposes, permission would have to be obtained from the copyright holder. Obviously, this was not practical. Without fair use, the restrictions on copyright would severely limit the educational uses of *all* the material created by others. The goal of fair use is to avoid the rigid application of the copyright statute when it would stifle the very creativity the law was meant to foster.

Fair use is controversial in that it is a contradiction of the basic concept of copyright's five rights. Fair use provides the privilege of using an author's work without permission or payment. In 1978, the new copyright act spelled out fair use—but only after resistance. The copyright committee working on the new law felt that trying to nail down specific guidelines for fair use in an era of technological change was futile. This was prophetic given that it was 1976 and the explosion of digital technology was still ten years away. However, the law was passed with fair use guidelines and later, in 1998, the Digital Millennium Copyright Act (DMCA) refined fair use as applied to a digital environment (see the section on the DMCA in chapter 4.)

The codification of fair use is short and seemingly straightforward in the text of the law, but this still does not make its application any clearer than in the past. As stated in the preceding chapter, copyright grants privileges upon a work's creation if that work is fixed in a tangible form. The work does not need to bear the copyright symbol or be registered. Thus, virtually anything written or available on the Internet is copyrighted.

Four factors in the law help guide those who wish to utilize its fair use aspects. As these factors are explained here, bear in mind that although fair use is spelled out, it is still not clear. It is also very difficult to explain fair use because for every concept presented, there is an exception or an immediate response from the reader of "But what if . . . ?" The four guiding factors are:

1. *The* purpose *and character of the use, including whether such use is of a commercial nature or is for nonprofit educational purposes*

   The courts have found that the use of a copyrighted work for educational purposes is the most likely application of the fair use statute. Outside educational purposes, any *noncommercial* use is likely to be looked upon as fair use if that use is "transformative." A work is transformative if it is based on the copyrighted work but adds some new element or has a different character or serves a different purpose. An example of this would be a parody or a satire of an existing work. So, a *noncommercial* parody of a song would be fair use.

   An example of fair use for educational purposes is a situation in which a professor makes a few copies of an article to be held on reserve in the library. The library already owns the material and is simply making allowances for time constraints of the students. The professor could copy an article on a given topic for each member of a class if securing authorization would require an unreasonable length of time, and if the article was used one time only and was returned by each student after use. The professor could not use the article as part of the curriculum from semester to semester unless permission from the author was secured. In this example, one can see how the fair use statute seems to say that a given act is permitted, but then limits how permitted it is.

2. *The nature of the copyrighted work*

The gist of this guideline concerns how the work is to be used. For example, a how-to book on woodworking contains plans that are to be copied and used by the reader. It is assumed that the reader is not going to take the book into the workshop and prop it open on the workbench. The physical nature of the work is significant in this guideline.

Nonfiction works have received more leeway in fair use than fiction in court cases involving fair use. The issue seems to be that nonfiction simply relates facts whereas fiction reflects true creative inspiration. A health workbook with tear-out pages for doing assignments would not be a good candidate for fair use if a teacher made copies of the consumable pages. An article from a textbook would be a good candidate for fair use. Audiovisual works or software are not good candidates for fair use.

3. *The amount and substantiality of the portion used in relation to the copyrighted work as a whole*

One hundred words taken from an encyclopedia for educational purposes may be fair use, but one hundred words taken from a children's book may not be. The guideline concerns not the volume of material alone, but what portion of the entire work the excerpt constitutes. Even though the amount of material used may be small, if it is deemed to constitute a significant part of the whole or is substantial in terms of importance, it is not permitted. So, how much is significant? The answer is not clear and, in many cases, the courts have had to decide how much is too much in a given situation. That is, even if a small amount of a short story is used, if it is considered the heart of the story, it is not permitted.

Some universities have tried to give rules of thumb concerning the amount of material that may be used under fair use guidelines. For example, Penn State University is very specific in its guidelines for fair use of prose. Penn State's Copyright Clearance Center states that a complete article up to 2,500 words may be used, or an excerpt from any prose work of not more than 1,000 words or 10 percent of the work, whichever is less, but in any event a minimum of 500 words. If the material to be copied is poetry, only 250 words may be used for educational fair use; if it is a children's book, no more than 10 percent of the text may be used; and if it is an illustration, a diagram, a drawing, a cartoon, or a picture, only one per work is considered fair use.

4. *The effect of the use upon the potential market for or value of the copyrighted work*

This is perhaps the better-understood concept of fair use. If the use of a copyrighted article impacts significantly on the potential of that work to provide a monetary profit to its author, the use is infringement and not fair use. In educational settings, a professor would be permitted to make copies of a work for nonprofit use if *all four* fair use guidelines are followed. A professor could not make photocopies of a worksheet from a single purchased workbook for all the students in the class. This would be detrimental to the market potential of the original work.

Note that all four factors carry equal weight in determining fair use. That is, *all four* factors are considered in each case of determining fair use, not just one or two of the factors. If a professor uses copyrighted material for educational, nonprofit purposes, that does not mean the professor need not be concerned about the amount used.

These factors reflect the balancing act that fair use requires. No litmus test exists for uses that are to be considered fair under copyright law; however, educators and librarians can be somewhat confident because courts award damages on the proof that actual loss has occurred because of infringement. If no economic gain is realized, even though infringement may be proven, damage awards may not be given to the copyright holder. A court would rule that infringement occurred and that the action must stop, but would not monetarily punish the offender outside of legal costs.

Even so, some educators demonstrate a bifurcated approach to the fair use doctrine. On one hand, educators often try to excuse infringement when acquiring permission seems too time-consuming and difficult. On the other hand, educators often give up legal fair use in the face of perceived litigation.

Classroom use is not the only time educators confront the issue of fair use. Fair use is also a factor in professional education programs, fund-raising, and alumni activities. For librarians, fair use becomes an issue when copyrighted material enters the interlibrary loan system, when material is placed on library reserve, or when articles are downloaded from full-text databases.

FAIR USE ISSUES FOR LIBRARIANS

In the current environment, librarians are faced with myriad issues concerning materials that are digitized. The best way to explain fair use for librarians is to look at specific examples of situations in which librarians may find themselves. There are several important points to keep in mind. The first point is that although fair use is involved in many library copyright situations, licensing and contract law also come into play because many of the digital products libraries use are purchased through a contractual agreement with a vendor. The second important point is that the Digital Millennium Copyright Act (DMCA) affects librarians if the library is acting as an Internet service provider (ISP). An ISP is an entity that provides the technology that allows users to exchange information electronically or to share files. America Online (AOL), for example, is an ISP. The best way to determine if a library is an ISP is to look at the URL (uniform resource locator). If the Web address is the library itself, the library is the ISP. If the library is only one location on a university or community domain, the library is not the ISP.

The Fair Use List of Factors

The chart shown in figure 3.1 may assist librarians and educators in making decisions on whether fair use is permissible in a given situation. This list may be used for any consideration of fair use, whether it involves digital media or other formats. The list may be considered a balance sheet in that the selection of one favorable item or one unfavorable item does not in itself permit or exclude fair use, but rather points to the pros and cons of a given situation. The final decision still rests in the hands of the educator or librarian.

Passing into the Public Domain

The one sure way to determine whether a work can be used under fair use guidelines is to determine whether the copyright on the work has expired. This is referred to as *passing into the public domain*. Two issues must be considered when determining whether a work is in the public domain.

FIGURE 3.1
Fair Use Factors

Fair Use Would Be Permitted If the Purpose Is:
Educational
Nonprofit
News
Criticism
Parody or Satire
"Transformative"

Fair Use Would Not Be Permitted If the Purpose Is:
Commercial
For Profit
For Entertainment

Fair Use Would Be Permitted If the Nature of the Work Is:
Published
Nonfiction

Fair Use Would Not Be Permitted If the Nature of the Work Is:
Unpublished
Creative (e.g., music or film)
Fiction

Fair Use Would Be Permitted If the Amount Used Is:
Small
Central to the work

Fair Use Would Not Be Permitted If the Amount Used Is:
Large
Not central to the work

Fair Use Would Be Permitted If:
The work is lawfully acquired (i.e., purchased)
There is no way to obtain permission
Few copies are available
There is no impact on profit
No similar product is available

Fair Use Would Not Be Permitted If:

Numerous copies are made

There is repeated use

The profit of the copyrighted work is affected

The work is easily licensed

The work is available on the Internet

First, although a work is very old, the copyright date on the work itself must be checked. For example, *Tom Sawyer* was published in 1869. Clearly there should be no copyright protection on this work because it is over 130 years old. But there is. Publishers can release a reedited version of a work or a version that is annotated or in paperback or one that has text that makes it different from the original. In this way the reedited or changed book can be copyrighted again with all the contents, including the text that was in the original publication, protected by a new copyright.

The second issue involves determining which of the several copyright laws the work falls under. There have been several major copyright acts in the United States in the past century, each with different periods of protection. The problem is to determine which of the protection periods applies to the work in hand. To make this determination a bit easier, figure 3.2 lists protection periods for works created under each copyright law.

FIGURE 3.2

Copyright Protection Periods

If the work was created:

Before 1923

The term of protection is:

In the public domain

If the work was created:

1923–1963

The term of protection is:

28 years plus renewal for 47 years (plus another 20 years provided by the Sonny Bono Act of 1998) making total protection time 95 years. If not renewed, protection expires after 28 years.

(continued)

FIGURE 3.2

Copyright Protection Periods (continued)

If the work was created:

1964–1977

The term of protection is:

28 years plus renewal for 67 years

If the work was created:

1978 and after

The term of protection is:

The life of the author plus 70 years. If a work has multiple authors, the protection under the most recent law (1976) is the life of the longest-living author plus 70 years. If the author is anonymous, or if the work is made for hire, the 1976 law protects the work for 95 years from the year of first publication or 120 years from the year of creation, whichever expires first.

Chapter 4

Napster, CONFU, and the DMCA

In 1988, a student at Northeastern University was pursuing his favorite pastime, locating and downloading MP3 files from the Internet. MP3 files are audio files that are compressed and sent over the Internet to others who can then download the files and play the music on their computers. The term *MP3* stems from a file compression format devised by the Motion Picture Expert Group. Not only could those receiving MP3s listen to the music, they could then send those MP3s to others or download them onto another medium, such as a CD.

The student, Matt, was having problems locating MP3s using the traditional web-based search engines like Yahoo! or Alta Vista. Matt discussed the problem with his roommate who was a computer science major. Matt's roommate, Shawn, became intrigued with the problem and in his spare time did some programming to resolve the problem of accurately and reliably locating MP3s.

Eventually, Shawn developed a small program that he gave to a select group of friends. Word of the program spread quickly, and soon Shawn realized that the demand for the program he had written could turn into a full-time job. Shawn Fanning decided to leave Northeastern and pursue a career that revolved around his software, known as Napster.

Napster (Fanning's nickname because of his "nappy" hair) is a simple program that allows a user to search the hard drive of another user for MP3 files. A user downloads Fanning's software from napster.com and installs it on her or his computer. Once the software is installed, the user enters the name of a song or an artist and sends that request to Napster, which looks for other computer users who have installed the Napster software and have the requested song on their hard drives. Napster sends the list of users with the requested song back to the original requester, who can then choose one of the listings of the song and have that song copied on her or his hard drive. The song can then be played through the computer or copied to a CD or to an MP3 player.

Napster makes downloading of MP3s simple and also makes possible the customization of CDs with songs by many artists. The advantage of being able to download MP3 files is that people can listen to just one song without having to spend $20 for a CD. Users can find music that they couldn't find elsewhere, including music that is no longer available for sale.

There are major problems with Napster that apply to the world of intellectual property. Downloading music for personal enjoyment is allowed under the 1992 Audio Home Recording Act, which allows the copying of music from a CD to a tape so that the music can be used in, say, an automobile without a CD player. These personal uses are considered fair use. (See chapter 3 on fair use.) Napster maintains that its software enables fair use of recorded music, and it also claims that Napster's use as a tool to promote music artists' work outweighs its potential use as a means of pirating music. After all, the video recorder was viewed in much the same way after its introduction, and Sony was sued to stop the manufacture of its machine, whose primary purpose was to duplicate videotapes. In the Sony case the court ruled that the legal uses of the recorder outweigh the possible illegal uses by those unlawfully copying videotapes for resale or distribution. The primary complaint against Napster is that the very purpose of the software is to allow users to obtain music without paying for it—to pirate copyrighted songs.

Several issues are at the heart of the Napster controversy. As a fair use issue, it is unique because traditionally there has never been a situation regarding fair use in which the costs to distribute a copyrighted work are nonexistent. Also traditionally, whenever a new technology comes into popular use, a cry arises that traditional copyright principles are outmoded. Even with the advent of the Digital Millennium Copyright Act, which attempts to address some of the issues involving the Internet and copyright, some believe that technology is outpacing the ability of the law to regulate it. The well-worn "guns don't kill people; people kill people" slogan also has been applied to Napster. Napster itself isn't illegal. It's the people who use it for illegal purposes who are at fault.

The challenge of technology has always been an uphill battle for intellectual property law. The VCR, the photocopy machine, and motion pictures have all created their share of copyright controversy. In the early part of the twentieth century, the issue was whether the copyright protection that included sheet music extended to a new invention—the piano roll. The cylinders with scatterings of holes were nothing like the legible, copyrightable sheet music, although they served the same purpose as a tool to allow music to be heard. But composers and publishers saw the piano roll as a device that would cut into their profits. The case made it to the Supreme Court in 1908. The Court rejected the publishers' argument. In the Copyright Act of 1909, lawmakers were careful to include piano rolls as items covered by copyright protection as well as protection for another new device—the phonograph.

Seven decades later, in 1976, a new copyright law attempted to address some issues related to technology and intellectual property. The new law expanded the duration of protection to the life of the author plus fifty years and codified for the first time the factors to be considered in deciding fair use. The new law, however, provided no guidance on how to weigh those factors.

The problem of determining infringement when a photocopy machine is used emerged in the 1960s in a dispute between the federal government and the Williams and Wilkins Company, a publishing firm. The governmental agency involved was the National Library of Medicine, which had a practice of freely copying articles from journals for patrons. When Williams and Wilkins heard of this practice, it asked the library to pay two cents per page for the articles it was duplicating, claiming that the practice affected the profit potential for the journals being copied. The library refused to pay, so, in 1968, the case was filed in the U.S. Court of Claims. The National Library of Medicine claimed that the photocopying practice constituted fair use because the copies were for scholarly use. In 1973 the U.S. Court of Claims agreed. The case was then taken to the Supreme Court, which heard arguments in 1974. The Justices ruled 4–4 on the case, with one Justice recused. This tie vote let the Court of Claims ruling stand in favor of the library.

In 1976, the new copyright law addressed this issue. The new law provided that libraries could reproduce a single copy of a work if the copy was not intended for commercial purposes. The new law also allowed libraries to make copies for interlibrary loan, provided the copies did not substitute for a subscription to a journal. The 1976 law also absolved libraries of liability for patrons' use of photocopy machines to copy journals as long as a notice was posted near the machines warning of copyright protections.

The VCR issue arose just before the 1976 copyright law was passed. In November 1976, Universal City Studios sued Sony Corporation in federal court. The issue was that the then dominant videocassette recorder, the Sony Betamax (now defunct), allowed the public to freely copy televised motion pictures, which affected the studio's ability to charge broadcasters for repeated showings of the films. Sony was sued for contributory infringement, which meant that Sony was not actually performing illegal copying, but was enabling others to do so.

Once again, after decisions for each party in the lower courts, the case made its way to the Supreme Court. In 1984, the Court decided that because most of the copying being done was for the purpose of time shifting—taping a program to view at a different time—it constituted fair use because it was a noncommercial use and had no effect on the market for the program. In reality, the decision was a boon for the movie studios. Video rental now produces over half the revenue for a given motion picture.

The current controversy relating to Napster is very similar to these other cases. The same problem—technology making possible acts that were not foreseen in the law—is evident in the Napster situation. The claim of publishers and producers that the technology impacts the profit potential and control of distribution is present as is the public's cry that making a copy for one's own use is fair use.

Those in favor of Napster make the following points. First, Napster is legal because the conduct of the users is legal. Users engage in person-to-person, nonprofit sharing of music. This right is granted in the 1992 Audio Home Recording Act, which allows the public to make copies of purchased music on other media—"space shifting"—for personal use. For example, a person may copy a song from a legally purchased CD to an audiotape so the song can be played in a car without a CD player.

Second, like the VCR, Napster is capable of performing a number of functions that are legal and useful. Because one person uses the service to engage in unlawful activities does not make Napster itself illegal. Napster cannot control the activities of its users in the same way a gun manufacturer cannot control the activities of those who purchase one of its guns. This concept of not being liable for the contributory infringement (one of the issues in the VCR decision) is spelled out in the Digital Millennium Copyright Act, passed in October 1998.

The size of Napster (at its peak, 58 million people had downloaded Napster software) makes it possible for lesser-known musicians to have broad distribution of their art. In 2000, over 25,000 artists authorized Napster to share their music.

Finally, Napster allows users to preview music before purchasing a CD. It also allows users to locate out-of-print or obscure music that is impossible to obtain otherwise.

Those not in favor of Napster, specifically the Recording Industry Association of America (RIAA), make the following points. First, the basis of Napster's software is to allow trafficking in stolen, copyrighted works. Unlike users who time shift television programs by videotaping them for later viewing, Napster users create permanent collections of music that has been unlawfully duplicated and distributed. That practice reduces revenue and reduces sales of CDs. Other services are available that legally allow the downloading of copyrighted music files under a subscription model.

Second, the revenue lost in the unlawful duplication and distribution not only affects the recording industry, but also devalues creativity itself by severely limiting the reward for a creative work. Although Napster may have some beneficial uses, these are not enough to outweigh its primary unlawful purpose. The widespread use of Napster has led to an attitude by the general population that there is no harm in stealing the inspiration for and the fruits of one's creativity.

Currently, Napster has appealed a decision to shut down its service and has agreed to remove all copyrighted music from its central server. The number of users of Napster has dropped dramatically, and most major universities prohibit the software on university-owned networks. In addition, several companies have announced plans to launch Napster-like services. The new services will be subscription-based, allowing users to download MP3s in the same manner as was possible through Napster but requiring a monthly fee or a rate for each song downloaded.

CONFERENCE ON FAIR USE (CONFU)

In an attempt to deal with issues regarding technology and education, a group of librarians, publishers, educators, technical experts, and others met in 1994 with then Secretary of Commerce Ron Brown. The group, calling itself the Conference on Fair Use (CONFU), attempted to generate a set of fair use guidelines for various electronic formats, including the Internet. Such issues as digital imaging, electronic reserves in libraries, distance learning, production of multimedia, and interlibrary loan were open for discussion. CONFU issued a draft document with proposed guidelines in 1997. The guidelines were met with a mixed response.

The CONFU guidelines are not law. Rather, they represent an agreement among the organizations that have created them and endorsed them. After three years of discussion, the CONFU members could not reach full agreement over the proposed guidelines, so some organizations support the guidelines and some do not. No major library organization has endorsed the CONFU guidelines. The major problem with the guidelines is that although the right questions and issues were brought to the table, the answers could not satisfy the diverse needs and concerns of the various groups who convened to draft them.

For example, one of the CONFU guidelines states that electronic course reserves must be limited to students enrolled in a given class and that access must be restricted by use of a password that would be known only to the students in that class. In smaller or financially limited educational institutions, where technological means to restrict access to electronic reserves are not available, CONFU allows access without a password for fifteen days. Some CONFU members were concerned that enrolled students would not keep a password confidential and would allow access to others outside the class and concerns that not limiting access by password would allow free access by nonstudents.

In no way should these guidelines be considered a safe harbor for those weighing the issues of fair use for digital works. The guidelines do represent a purposeful attempt to apply fair use to a given situation involving digital works when a definitive answer is not available. In looking at incidents of infringement, the courts historically have looked at the concept of "due diligence." That is, if infringement has occurred, is it because of the reckless theft of known copyrighted works or is the infringement the result of an error by a party that has attempted to make a deliberate decision under the concept of fair use? If a librarian or an educator follows the guidelines, although the guidelines are not law, they may point the user in the correct direction. Be warned that the following information is only a summary of the more significant CONFU guidelines. The complete CONFU report can be found at http://www.uspto.gov/web/offices/dcom/olia/confu.

CONFU Guidelines

- In distance-education situations in which information is transmitted over the Internet to enrolled students, there must be "technological limitations" on the students' ability to access the information. This means that only enrolled students can access the information by using a password or a PIN number. For example, access to items placed on electronic reserve must be restricted by password to only those enrolled in a given class.

- Educators may make available to students via the Internet a presentation that they have given to peers, such as a workshop or conference presentation.
- Educators may retain multimedia projects in their personal portfolios for later personal uses, such as a tenure review.
- Educators may use their educational multimedia projects for a period of up to two years after the first use with a class. Use beyond that period, even for educational purposes, requires permission for each copyrighted portion incorporated in the production.
- Up to 10 percent or three minutes, whichever is less, of a copyrighted motion media work may be reproduced or otherwise incorporated as part of a multimedia project for educational purposes.
- Up to 10 percent or 1,000 words, whichever is less, of a copyrighted work consisting of text material may be reproduced or otherwise incorporated as part of a multimedia project. An entire poem of less than 250 words may be used, but no more than three poems by one poet or five poems by different poets from a single anthology may be used.
- Up to 10 percent, but in no event more than thirty seconds, of the music and lyrics from an individual musical work may be reproduced or otherwise incorporated as part of a multimedia project.
- A photograph or illustration may be used in its entirety, but no more than five images by an artist or a photographer may be reproduced as part of an educational multimedia project. When using photographs and illustrations from a published collective work, not more than 10 percent or fifteen images, whichever is less, may be reproduced.
- Up to 10 percent or 2,500 fields or cell entries, whichever is less, from a copyrighted database or data table may be reproduced or otherwise incorporated as part of an educational multimedia project. A "field or cell entry" is either a name or a social security number or the intersection where a row and a column meet on a spreadsheet.
- No more than two use copies may be made of an educator's multimedia project, and only one copy may be placed on reserve in a library. An additional copy may be made for preservation purposes,

but it may only be used or copied to replace a copy that has been lost, stolen, or damaged.

- Educators must credit the sources used in all multimedia projects used for educational purposes.

As stated earlier, these guidelines are not law. Librarians and educators can use them as a reasonable guide in deciding instances of fair use for educational purposes when using electronic media. However, the best course is to apply the guidelines for fair use (see chapter 3).

THE DIGITAL MILLENNIUM COPYRIGHT ACT

Although the CONFU guidelines are not law, the Digital Millennium Copyright Act (DMCA) is law. During 1998, the 105th Congress passed two bills to amend the 1976 Copyright Act: the Sonny Bono Copyright Term Extension Act and the DMCA. The Copyright Term Extension Act extends the period of copyright protection by twenty years. Sonny Bono, a congressman from the Palm Springs district of California and a former music performer, producer, and composer, sponsored this legislation. He felt that this legislation was needed because some of the music created in the early days of the rock and roll era would soon fall into the public domain under the 1976 Copyright Law. Under the 1976 law, the duration of copyright is the life of the creator plus fifty years. Because a number of prominent artists had died at a young age in the 1950s and 1960s, it was feared that as early as the first decade of the twenty-first century, their music, which was still very popular, would pass into the public domain while it was still a source of significant income for the descendants of the artists. By adding twenty years to the term of copyright protection, the fruits of these deceased artists' creativity could still provide income to their families.

The DMCA is not a new copyright law, but rather an addendum to the Copyright Law of 1976 that attempts to address some of the issues of copyright and the Internet. Important items in this law greatly affect librarians and educators. The DMCA makes it a crime to circumvent antitheft devices built into software to protect it from piracy. For example, if a faculty member places items on electronic reserve for a given class and protects these items with a password that is known only to members of her class, it is illegal for a librarian to circumvent that password so that the reserve items can be used by others. Or, if an instructor purchases software that has built-in protections to prohibit downloading of the text or images, it would be illegal for the instructor to devise a means or to write additional software that would allow others to download images from the protected software.

Along these same lines, the sale or manufacture of devices used to illegally copy protected software is illegal. It is legal, however, for a university faculty member to conduct research into how to break copyright protection devices. The DMCA also allows nonprofit libraries and educational institutions *under certain specific circumstances* to circumvent protection devices and software.

The DMCA also limits the liability of an Internet service provider (ISP) when one of its customers violates copyright law. This particular issue had been the subject of significant court cases. At the heart of this concept is the liability of an ISP, such as AOL or a university domain, if the ISP did not have knowledge of the illegal activity. In some previous court cases, providing the means to perform illegal activity under copyright law constituted contributory infringement. Under the DMCA, even if the ISP made available the technology to pirate copyrighted works that appear on the Internet, the ISP is not liable if it had no knowledge of the illegal activity *under certain circumstances*.

For example, in order to be an ISP, the provider must register with the Copyright Office. This action requires the provider to name a designated "agent" who acts as a contact in cases of infringement. Virtually all colleges and universities that maintain a network for the scholarly and informational needs of the academic community would be considered ISPs. It would follow that in order to be protected from liability with regard to the DMCA, all colleges and universities and large school systems would have to identify an agent. In this way, a small operation may not designate itself as an ISP in an attempt to hide behind the DMCA in protecting itself from liability.

In addition, the DMCA spells out four ways in which the ISP is involved or not involved with infringing material. First, there is no liability for an ISP if it is involved with simple transitory communications—that is, if the ISP is acting as a conduit for information and not providing content itself. Second, the ISP is not liable in cases of system caching in which the ISP *temporarily* saves information for easy access. That is, it allows the subscriber to repeatedly get information without contacting the original source. Third, an ISP is not liable if it acts as a web page host and agrees to post notices of take down (see the following section). Finally, an ISP is not liable under the DMCA if it provides location tools, such as links to other sites, as long as it agrees to abide by take-down procedures. The point is that although it seems as if the DMCA is protecting ISPs against any liability in cases of infringement, the instances in which protection occurs are quite specific.

Notice and Take Down

A disturbing feature of the DMCA involves what is called "notice and take down provisions." The best way to explain this feature of the DMCA is with an example. Mr. Smith notices that his copyrighted photograph of a dog appears on the website of a company that sells dog toys, DogEToys. Mr. Smith has not licensed or permitted DogEToys to use his photograph. Mr. Smith sends a written notification to USOnline, the ISP on which the offending photograph appears, stating that the photograph appears without his permission. According to the DMCA, USOnline is required to "expeditiously" remove or block access to the offending page. By doing this, USOnline is exempt from any liability from the copyright holder, Mr. Smith, or the web page owner, DogEToys.

Once the offending material has been removed by USOnline, USOnline has to take additional steps to protect the rights of DogEToys. In what are termed "notice and put back procedures," USOnline must take "reasonable steps" to notify DogEToys that the web page has been removed from USOnline's servers. DogEToys then must either send a counter notice to USOnline stating that the material in question was legal or was misidentified as nonlicensed information or accept the removal of the offending material.

If such counter notice is sent, to remain exempt from liability, USOnline must then provide a copy of this statement to Mr. Smith. After receiving this statement, Mr. Smith must notify USOnline that a court action has been initiated. If USOnline receives no notice from Mr. Smith that a court action is imminent, USOnline must put back the offending material in no less than ten days but not more than fourteen days to escape liability.

The disturbing part of these notice and take down provisions is that material can be removed from the Internet for ten to fourteen days simply because of an accusation by a copyright holder who may or may not have any evidence that copyright infringement has actually occurred. In such situations as the preceding example, where a commercial website selling goods is shut down, the monetary damage could be significant; however, the ISP is immune from liability if it follows the procedures set forth in the DMCA. In no other area of law may a person's source of income be cut off simply on the basis of an accusation of one party. Nor may a person be left with restrictions on the possibility of suing one of the offending parties.

Normally, in United States law, evidence must be produced before any action is taken to limit the First Amendment rights of any party.

In summary, the issues of copyright and the Internet are not ephemeral. The problems of new technology have always been a part of copyright law and its interpretation. The problems that accompany Napster-like services, which allow easy copying of protected property, will occur repeatedly as changes in technology make obsolete the safeguards placed on them. Groups representing copyright holders, industry, artists, librarians, and educators will continue to prepare guidelines for the safe use and handling of intellectual property in the digital age. Finally, a new copyright law will be passed that incorporates the significant changes in technology into the protection and fair use of available information for all.

Chapter 5

Intellectual Property and the Courts

Over the past two hundred years, legal cases have helped interpret the complicated issues surrounding copyright protection. In many of these cases, the decision reached determined all future application of copyright law. The following review highlights the points of law that made each of these cases significant in the application of copyright in the United States.

COPYRIGHT AND THE INTERNET

To date, no court cases have tested the legality of certain aspects of copyright as it applies to the Internet. For example, the public "broadcast" of a play over the Internet by a teacher without limiting access to members of a class has not been challenged. The DMCA has tried to address some of the concerns that arise from electronic media. In pre-DMCA court cases in which electronic media were an issue in copyright disputes, the courts applied the traditional principles of copyright law to the new technologies in predictable ways. For example, the fact that a work appears on a website does not give license to a viewer of that work to copy it. Courts have not hesitated to rule that copying a work in a computer's random access memory, even if a temporary copy, is more than transitory use and constitutes a reproduction subject to control of the copyright holder (*MAI Systems Corp. v. Peak Computer, Inc.*, 991 F. 2d 511, 519). Uploading and downloading of copyrighted works outside the framework of fair use have consistently been found to be infringements (*Playboy Enterprises v. Frena*, 839 F. Supp. 1552).

COPYRIGHT AND DIFFERING MEDIA

How the courts perceive the distinction between media and copyright was demonstrated by the Supreme Court in the case of *Mazer v. Stein* in 1954. Stein created molded statuettes and registered the design as a nonutilitarian "work of art" under the copyright law. Mazer copied the statuette design and, by drilling holes in the top and bottom and wiring the sculpture, rendered the statuette a functional lamp. Mazer argued that because the work of art was functional in its use as a lamp base and was in a different medium, the copyright law would no longer protect Stein.

The Court ruled in favor of Stein and held that even though a functionally useless item could be rendered functional, that action cannot negate protection of the functionless sculpture under copyright law. This case demonstrates that the concepts of copyright law apply to all media; that is, a change in the manner in which an expression is "fixed in a tangible medium" does not alter the law. This concept was very important in the copyright cases that occurred after *Mazer v. Stein* and especially important in regard to copyright as it applies to the Internet. The fact that the medium has changed does not change the application of the law. That is, although it is simple and easy to copy text, pictures, and other elements from a website, that alone does not make unauthorized copying of protected works legal.

King Features v. Kleeman in 1941 demonstrates the concept of copyright protection as it applies only to the specific thing being protected. King Features copyrighted "Popeye the Sailor" originally as a comic strip, a two-dimensional graphic work of art. Kleeman used the two-dimensional comic strip drawings as a guide in manufacturing three-dimensional Popeye dolls. Once again, the alleged infringer maintained that changing the medium in which the copying takes place alters the application of copyright law. However, King Features claimed infringement of copyright because the dolls were essentially copies of a protected Popeye drawing.

King Features won the decision, but barely. Only after King Features' attorneys were able to show that the alleged infringements were duplicates of actual copyrighted drawings did the decision swing in their favor. Had Kleeman made the dolls from a Popeye drawing that Kleeman had created himself instead of one that had been copied from a published Popeye cartoon, the decision may have been in Kleeman's favor. The fact that the

Popeye dolls were an *exact* copy of a drawing proved infringement. In the digital world the concept is the same—a protected drawing or picture taken from the Internet may not be used in the creation of another work of art in a different medium.

COPYRIGHT AND INTERNET SERVICE PROVIDERS

The responsibilities of Internet service providers (ISPs) have been explored in several cases. In 1994, the first case involving an ISP, *MAI v. Peak*, established the definition of "copy" as it applies to electronic media. In this landmark decision, the court determined that the simple act of loading software into a computer's RAM is considered making a copy under the copyright law (*MAI Systems Corp. v. Peak Computer, Inc.*, 991 F. 2d 511, 519). In a related case, *Marobie-FL v. NAFED*, the court further determined that the length of time copies remain in RAM is irrelevant. There is no safe time to perform a copying procedure before it is deemed infringement.

Other cases have implied liability for ISPs and bulletin board service (BBS) operators. In *Playboy Enterprises v. Frena*, a BBS that contained copyrighted pictures owned by *Playboy* was found liable even though the BBS operator did not make the copies himself and was proven not to have known about the existence of them on his BBS as the servers work automatically. In effect, the BBS operator was liable for merely providing a means by which to make copies. If this logic were extended, ISPs could be held liable for the activities of their users. However, this case was decided before the Digital Millennium Copyright Act (DMCA) attempted to sort out the responsibilities of ISPs in copyright matters.

The copyright responsibilities of ISPs for the activities of others was further explored in a 1995 case involving the *Religious Technology Center v. Netcom* (907 F. Supp. 1361; 1995 U.S. Dist. LEXIS 18173). Files containing copyrighted materials owned by the Church of Scientology were placed on an Internet newsgroup through a server controlled by Netcom. The user who placed the files actually used a local bulletin board system (BBS) that provided Internet access through Netcom. The church wanted the material removed from Netcom servers. When Netcom refused to remove the materials, the church went to court.

The court found that neither Netcom nor the BBS had directly infringed on copyright because neither party took any action to cause copies to be made. Although the church received no monetary reward, the court found that Netcom may be liable for contributory infringement by materially contributing to infringement by the Internet user. The court stated that if Netcom knew about the copyrighted materials on its server, it should have removed them. Before a decision was made in this case, however, the parties settled out of court. It is also significant that this case took place before the DMCA took effect in 1998.

Cases decided since *Netcom* have followed the same analysis. A BBS operator who knowingly allowed users to upload and download copyrighted SEGA video games was determined not to be a direct infringer, but because the operator knew about the activity, he was guilty of contributory infringement.

DIGITAL PLAGIARISM

A 1996 case between the Long Island newspaper *Newsday* and a photography agency is one of the first involving what is termed *digital plagiarism* of an image nearly too small to see. The case involved a photomontage, a large photograph made of thousands of tiny photographs. A *Newsday* illustrator had copied, without permission, a photo by James Porto as part of a larger computer-generated photomontage for the newspaper's cover page. The photo agency was awarded damages by the court.

Also in 1996, Adobe Photoshop's Image Club marketed a CD with images by Edward Hopper and Georgia O'Keeffe, among others. The image of Hopper's *Lighthouse* is owned by the Dallas Museum of Art and O'Keeffe's images are owned by the O'Keeffe Foundation. Adobe secured the images from a company called Planet Art. Adobe was assured by Planet Art that the images were royalty free even though the Hopper *Lighthouse* carried a copyright symbol. As the situation progressed, it was learned that Planet Art had simply scanned the images from an art catalog. Neither the Dallas museum nor the O'Keeffe Foundation was able to locate anyone associated with Planet Art. On receiving cease and desist letters from the Dallas museum, Adobe was forced to destroy 350 unsold CDs and had to inform previous buyers of the CD that the images on it were copyrighted and could not be used without permission.

THE DOCTRINE OF FIRST SALE

In the Adobe case the doctrine of First Sale comes into play. In the 1976 Copyright Law, (109a) First Sale is a concept that allows the owner of a lawfully obtained work the right to give or sell that copy to another without permission, but it does not allow the obtained work to be copied. For example, if a person buys a book, he or she may give *that* book to another person, but cannot make a *copy* of that book. If a person buys a painting, he or she may give or sell that painting to another, but may not make copies of the painting. Even though a painting is purchased, the copyright remains with the artist. Although the Dallas Museum of Art owned the rights to Hopper's *Lighthouse*, this is not always the case with works owned by museums. According to the First Sale doctrine, even though a museum may purchase a piece of art, it does not also purchase the right to reproduce or copy that piece of art unless the artist specifically grants that right to the purchaser. The sticking point here is that there is no clear agreement as to whether a display of a work on a remote computer is a permitted copy or a new copy being generated. Although copyright law permits a user to give another user a physical copy of a legally obtained book, the law prohibits a user from transmitting a digital copy of the same book without permission.

In 1998, a Los Angeles judge dismissed a copyright suit involving JC Penney and photographer Gary Bernstein (1998 U.S. Dist. LEXIS 19048). Bernstein sued Penney and cosmetics company Elizabeth Arden over a series of web links that led to an infringement of one of Bernstein's photographs. In 1997, Penney and Elizabeth Arden created a website that featured a photograph of actress Elizabeth Taylor. Taylor is the spokesperson for Elizabeth Arden's Passion perfume.

A link on the website led viewers to another site hosted by the Internet Movie Database, which in turn led viewers to a page produced in Sweden that carried Bernstein's unauthorized photograph of Taylor. The photograph in question had originally been produced in 1986 by Bernstein for the cover of a photography magazine. Bernstein had licensed the photograph to Arden for a publicity campaign. Bernstein maintained that in linking to other sites, Penney and Arden violated his rights to the picture's reproduction because the photograph was reproduced not only on the Penney site, but also on other sites that were linked to the Penney site, and Penney had knowingly allowed this to happen.

The defendant argued that a company whose product is merely displayed on another website cannot be held liable for any infringement by the author of that website. Linking does not constitute infringement because the server of the website does not process the content of the linked site. In its argument the defense cited the Netcom suit mentioned earlier as precedent for the protection of an ISP.

The case was dismissed because the defendant successfully argued that linking itself, although deliberate, is not infringement. The link acts as a gateway and not as a reproduction of the photo itself—that is, linking itself is not copying.

TRENDS

The pattern that emerges shows that the courts have used on a few landmark cases to begin to sort out the problems of copyright as it applies to electronic media. Many other aspects of copyright protection, such as whether audiovisual material on a website constitutes a "broadcast," have not been decided. In cases decided thus far, the courts have tended to treat electronic media as they would other media and have decided in favor of the copyright owner. This trend disturbs some because judgments consistently in favor of the copyright holders limit the fair use of electronic material for educational purposes. Although the DMCA has attempted to resolve some of these issues, this law seems to be driven by the publishing industry and the entertainment industry, which are seeking to protect their financial stake in the Internet at the risk of stifling legitimate access to information and the needs of education.

There are those who believe that the copyright law does not apply to electronic media, but historically, as new technologies such as film and television came along, the existing copyright law was shown to be applicable. Because Congress has seen fit to pass the DMCA, it is obvious that this new electronic medium does have some unique features that will be addressed in future court cases.

PATENTS AND THE COURT OF APPEALS

Before 1982, if a true inventor and holder of a patent took legal action against another who copied her patent without buying or licensing it, she had only a 50 percent chance of winning the suit. In 1982, a new Court of Appeals for the Federal Circuit, a specialized appellate court in Washington, D.C., was formed to deal exclusively with patent cases. This court not only hears patent cases exclusively, but also has taken a firmer stand on protecting the rights of the patent holder against infringement. Since that time, patent settlements in favor of the true patent holder have increased significantly, and the power of patent ownership has been strengthened, as was the case for Jerome Lemelson. At the same time, the new court has reeled in other cases it deemed to be frivolous, cases that previously had languished for years in lower courts before a decision was reached. For example, Mr. Lemelson lost a case involving his claim on the patent of Mattel's Hot Wheels toys because of frivolous claims that he had previously invented a miniature toy car.

Chapter 6

Patents

The right of individuals to hold patents is guaranteed by Article 1, Section 8 of the United States Constitution: "Congress shall have the power . . . to promote the progress of science and useful arts, by securing for limited times to authors and inventors the exclusive rights to their respective writings and discoveries."

Each of the creative properties of patents, copyrights, and trademarks requires by its nature its own set of laws and methods of control. Together these laws and practices form the subject of intellectual property. That is, the Constitution grants the rights of patent, copyright, and trademark protection, but the manner in which each is secured, the time frame allowed for protection, and other details are regulated by laws that were written later.

The framers of the Constitution realized that the right to exclude others from the rewards of an invention would be an incentive to create and would encourage business in the new nation. For the first time in the history of the world, a constitutional instrument recognized that individuals have a right to protect their intellectual property. Thomas Jefferson, the first patent commissioner, spoke of patents as "the locomotive that runs industry." Little did he know how important patents would become to the economy of the United States.

Most consumer goods that are offered on the open market are there because the manufacturer was able to gain an advantage over the competition by prohibiting others from copying a unique product. This may seem contrary to the concept of a free market, but the advantage given by intellectual property protection actually helps rather than hinders the economy. With a patent, an inventor can control the design, manufacture, licensing, distribution, and copying of inventions. A patent is, in effect, a temporary legal monopoly over a specific device or process.

The first patent in America was granted by the state of Massachusetts in 1641, 135 years before the founding of the United States. It was granted to Samuel Winslow for a unique process for manufacturing salt. The first patent on a mechanical device in the western hemisphere was issued to Joseph Jenkes in 1646 for a water-propelled machine that was used to manufacture scythes. In this invention a water wheel powered a hammer that beat metal into usable implements. Previously, scythes were manufactured by hand. The first United States patent was issued on July 31, 1790, to Samuel Hopkins for his new process of making potash, an ingredient in soap. In the first year of the U.S. system, Jefferson granted just three patents. Currently, about 70,000 patents are issued annually. Jefferson himself was an inventor and developed a revolving chair and a stool that could fold into a walking stick, although he never patented either device. One wag said that Jefferson invented the chair so that he could look all ways at once.

Until July 13, 1836, when a classification system was devised, patents were arranged alphabetically by the inventor's name and kept in wooden boxes. There were 9,957 patents granted up to that time. In 1836, the first numbered patent was granted to J. Ruggles for notched train wheels that permitted better traction on uphill grades.

As the first patent searcher, Jefferson insisted that patents be arranged in such a way that they could be researched easily. Jefferson kept drawings of his inventions in old wooden shoe boxes, and this became the standard filing system. A visitor to the Patent and Trademark Office (PTO) in Arlington, Virginia, can still see the millions of U.S. patents shelved in metal and wooden "shoes."

Few people are aware that during the Civil War, the Confederacy had its own patent office, headed by former Union patent examiner Rufus Rhodes. The Confederacy's first patent was issued on August 1, 1861, to James Houten for a breech-loading gun. The last Confederate patent, number 266, was issued on December 17, 1864, to W. Smith for a percussion cap rammer. Understandably, many of the Confederate patents were for war machines. The Confederate Patent Office was destroyed during the battle of Richmond in April 1865, and virtually all the models and records were lost, although some still exist in scattered private collections.

THE PATENT AND TRADEMARK OFFICE

The PTO is somewhat of an anachronism in the twenty-first century in that virtually the entire patenting process, from application to searching for existing patents, is performed manually. Recently, a large number of patents and drawings have been automated, and the chapters in this book on patent searching show ways in which a patent search can be done online. However, the traditional method of storing and searching patents on paper remains.

It is not a simple task to automate, digitize, and bring up to date the huge number of patents and their accompanying documentation. Not only do over 6 million patents have to be categorized and shelved, but also the approximately 165,000 patent applications that are submitted annually, along with hundreds of thousands of associated documents must be controlled. It is estimated that the PTO has a total of 30 million documents relating to patents and, according to the *Wall Street Journal*, at any given time nearly 2 million cannot be located. It is important that the PTO retain all these records because about 65 percent or seven in every eleven applications submitted to the PTO are eventually granted a patent, and accurate records are indispensable in case of an infringement suit. Patent examiners relate the story of a colleague who had run out of room in his office and stuffed so many patent applications in the suspended ceiling that the ceiling collapsed.

The government is willing to subsidize education for examiners, and many attend law school at night. Because the highest pay rate for an examiner is about $90,000 a year and patent attorneys can easily make $150,000 a year or more, many examiners let the government pay for their law degree and then leave the PTO to practice patent law.

As mentioned earlier, in recent years the PTO has embarked on a $1 billion project to automate the system. Some searching procedures have been automated and private vendors have made computerized databases of patents available. The PTO itself makes patents available online at www.uspto.gov. Appendix 2 lists additional online services as well as online sites that provide either patent text, drawings, or both.

SOME SUCCESSFUL PATENTS

An indication that the old manual filing system worked—at least for simple inventions—is that over the past two hundred years no other country could show a better record of innovation. The belief persists that a patent on a simple invention will make an individual rich and secure for the rest of his or her life. As Emerson reportedly said, "Build a better mousetrap and the world will beat a path to your door."

Sometimes this is true. In 1874, Joseph Glidden was granted patent 157,124 on barbed wire (see fig. 6.1). This revolutionary device permitted ranchers on the treeless plains to divide their ranch land effectively and economically. By 1887, 173,000 tons of barbed wire were being sold annually. In 1948, a Swiss engineer, George de Mestral, was annoyed by the tenacious grip of cockleburs on his socks after a hike. Looking at the burs under a microscope, he discovered that they were shaped like hundreds of tiny hooks that attached to the threads of his socks. De Mestral got a weaver in Lyon, France, to make a facsimile of the burs by hand. De Mestral improved on his original design, which he called "locking tape," and secured patents worldwide. His U.S. patent, 2,717,437, was granted in 1955 (see fig. 6.2), and, by the late 1950s, looms were turning out 60 million yards of Velcro annually.

Of course, not all patents are simple. In 1942, Chester Carlson was granted patent 2,297,691 on something called "electrophotography," a process that copied documents without the use of inks or liquids. An important point to remember is that a patent need only exist on paper. A model or prototype has not been required since the nineteenth century. Carlson had patented a *process*, not the actual machinery that would perform the process. Unable to convince anyone of the viability of the process, he assigned the patent rights in 1944 to the Battelle Memorial Institute in hopes that its researchers would build an electrophotography machine. Unable to do anything with the patent, Battelle offered an option to the Haloid Paper Company. Haloid executives felt that if they could develop a machine from Carlson's patent, they could sell more paper. Haloid developed the machine over the next thirteen years, changed the company's name to Xerox, and sold the first photocopy machine in 1962.

Because an invention only has to exist on paper, some very interesting applications have been submitted. The most interesting was an apparatus for keeping a severed human head alive. The PTO initially approved the "Device for Perfusing an Animal Head" application that was supported by four sketches and eleven pages of medical double-talk. It was later discovered that a patent lawyer sent it in as a joke.

Many companies obtain patents to control the technology of an entire industry and never intend to actually produce the product. Jerome Lemelson, a lone inventor who obtained patents in the 1950s on everything

FIGURE 6.1
Joseph Glidden's Patent for Barbed Wire

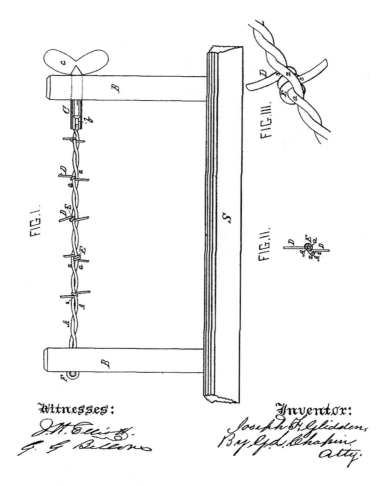

FIGURE 6.2

George de Mestral's Patent for Velcro

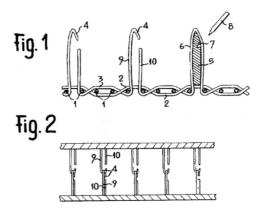

Sept. 13, 1955   G. DE MESTRAL   2,717,437

VELVET TYPE FABRIC AND METHOD OF PRODUCING SAME

Filed Oct. 15, 1952

INVENTOR

George de Mestral.

BY

ATTORNEY

from toys to computer vision technology, has earned over $200 million by threatening to sue automobile manufacturers for infringement on his patents. Japan's twelve leading car companies alone have paid over $100 million to Lemelson to settle out of court.

The classic case of industry control by patent ownership is that of the Selden auto patent. George Selden was a bright patent attorney who was also an amateur inventor. Fascinated with the concept of a self-propelled vehicle, Selden, in the late 1870s, developed and built a gasoline engine attached to a carriage. In his invention were the basic components of the automobile: a simple two-cycle engine, carriage, clutch, and running gear. It was hardly a marketable or practical vehicle, but on May 8, 1879, Selden applied for a patent.

Because Selden was a patent attorney and knew the status of patents under consideration at the PTO, he knew that his was the first patent application on an automobile. Selden managed to stall the patenting procedure by taking advantage of quirks in the system and was not granted patent 549,160 until November 5, 1895—sixteen years after his application (see fig. 6.3). During this time it was also possible to amend an application, which Selden did until his patent included virtually every major component of the automobile. It mattered not that during this time a superior four-stroke engine was developed or that Germany's Gottlieb Daimler was widely acclaimed as the true inventor of the practical motorcar; Selden was first in line. His patent would run seventeen years until 1912.

In 1899, fearing suit by Selden, a group of auto manufacturers approached him for a license because they could not produce any significant part of an automobile without infringing on Selden's patent. Selden approved and sat back and waited for the royalties to arrive. He made $200,000 because of his patent. He was challenged only by Henry Ford, who endured an eight-year court battle. Ford finally won the suit on appeal and broke Selden's monopoly in 1911, one year before the patent would have expired.

Edwin Land, inventor of the Polaroid camera, held patents on every component of the instant camera and on the process of instant development, prohibiting infringers from producing even minor subassemblies of his invention. It was only when Polaroid improved the camera or the film and introduced a new model that it allowed others to license its technology, but then others could only license older, obsolete models of an instant camera. Kodak, which lost a $909.5-million settlement to Polaroid, was found to be infringing on the process of instant photography by producing its own

FIGURE 6.3

George Selden's Patent for an Automobile

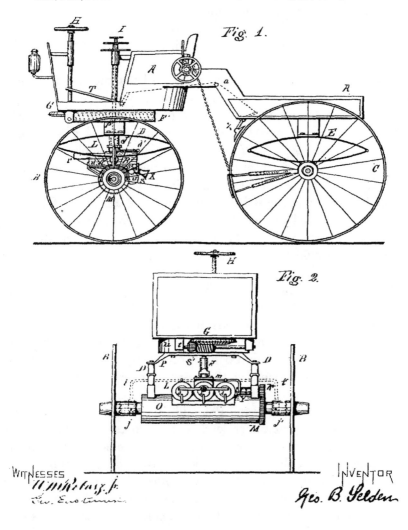

2 Sheets—Sheet 1.

G. B. SELDEN.
ROAD ENGINE.

No. 549,160.

Patented Nov. 5, 1895.

Fig. 1.

Fig. 2.

WITNESSES

INVENTOR

Geo. B. Selden

instant camera and film and was required to reimburse purchasers of its film and cameras with cash and coupons for other Kodak products.

A brilliant invention may be useless, however, without the technology to make it practical. Bell's telephone (patent 174,465; see fig. 6.4) required the additional inventions of switching devices, amplifiers, transformers, and transmission mechanisms. Once certain large patents are granted, a new company may be needed to obtain the capital support, management style, and technical expertise to make a truly great invention successful. Bell's invention, for example, gave birth to the Bell Telephone Company, but no better example illustrates this need for ancillary equipment and business acumen than Thomas Edison's electric light.

Edison did not invent the electric light in 1880. It was invented as early as 1838 when a French scientist passed an electric current through a carbon rod sealed inside a vacuum chamber and watched it glow. In 1878, two years before Edison was granted patent 223,898 (see fig. 6.5), Joseph Swan demonstrated a carbon filament vacuum lamp in England but did not patent it. There is evidence to suggest that Edison knew of Swan's discovery because Edison's Menlo Park library rivaled university research libraries of the time. Edison obtained a U.S. patent on the electric lamp, and when the British inventor attempted to put the electric light into production in the United States, Edison blocked Swan's efforts with litigation, charging that he owned the patent. Both men soon realized that the invention was useless without an electrical power source. Nobody would buy an electric light if there was no place in the house to plug it in. Edison and Swan dropped their legal action, joined forces, and formed the Edison & Swan Electric Company in 1883. By 1910, 3 million American homes were using electric light bulbs.

It is rarely the case that a simple or complex invention is successful; however, only about 65 percent of patent applications are approved, only about 10 percent are eventually marketed, and only 3 percent of patents issued ever make a dime for their inventors. The cost of obtaining a patent is usually outside the reach of a private inventor. Even if an inventor files a patent application *pro se* (on her or his own), the cost is generally several thousand dollars. Patent law is designed to encourage individual effort in that only individuals, not corporations, may be granted a patent; however, large companies with research and development divisions simply pay patenting fees and have the employee inventor assign the rights to the company. The process of selling a patent or of licensing a patent is a relatively simple matter and is discussed later in chapter 7.

FIGURE 6.4

Alexander Graham Bell's Patent for the Telephone

2 Sheets—Sheet 2.
A. G. BELL.
TELEGRAPHY.
No. 174,465.
Patented March 7, 1876.
Fig 6.
C
B
A
C'
B'
A'
e
g
Fig. 7
A
a
c
d
e
E
g
i
I
Witnesses
Inventor:
A. Graham Bell

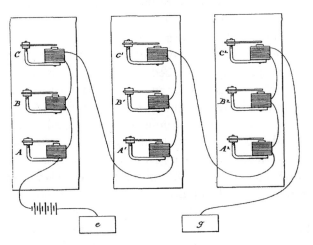

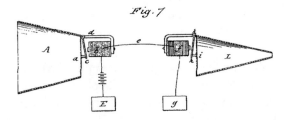

FIGURE 6.5
Thomas Edison's Patent for the Light Bulb

T. A. EDISON.
Electric-Lamp.

No. 223,898.   Patented Jan. 27, 1880.

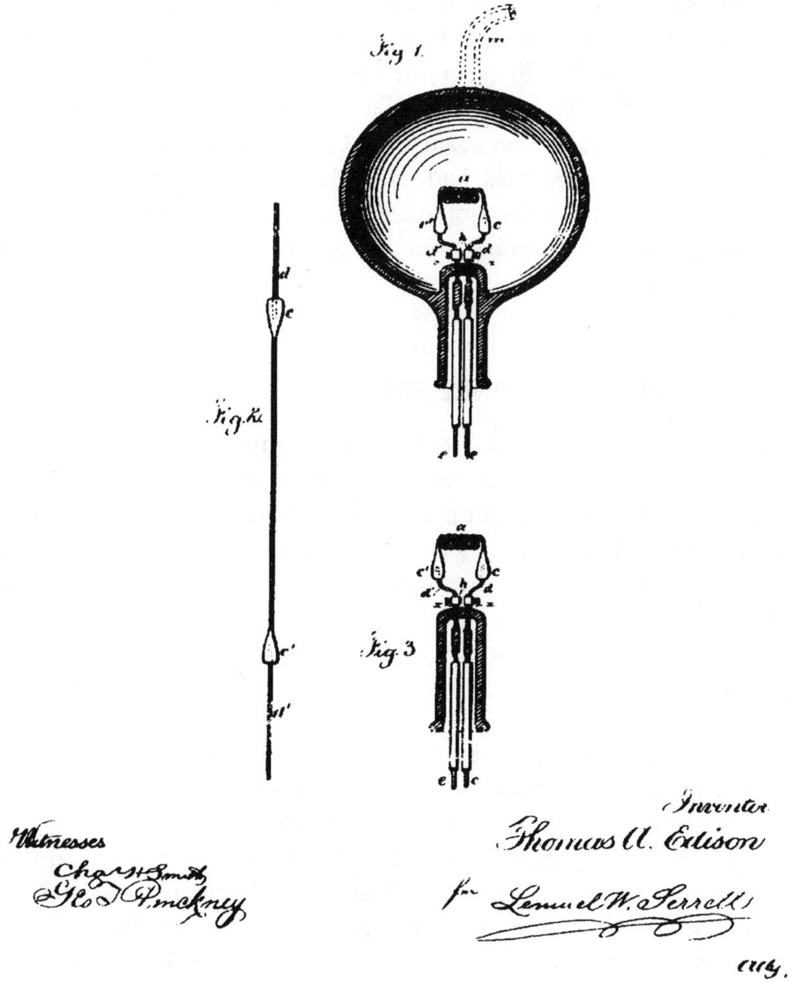

PATENT PROTECTION

U.S. patents are not an exclusive right of U.S. citizens. Citizens of any nation may patent their inventions in the United States. Foreign companies also often submit inventions for protection under U.S. patent laws and are often in competition with domestic companies for related inventions. U. S. companies are now competing with foreign companies, Japanese and German primarily, to obtain U.S. patents. Contrary to common belief, a U.S. patent offers no protection in other countries. For example, a patented U.S. invention may be produced by someone in Canada if the U.S. inventor has not secured a Canadian patent. The U.S. patent holder's only course of action, even if she or he had secured a Canadian patent, would be to initiate an expensive legal action against the Canadian infringer.

The preceding anecdotes and examples demonstrate several of the important foundations of the system. Before wading too deep into patenting, librarians should be familiar with the basic concepts and terms of patent law and processes.

PATENT TERMS AND CONCEPTS

A patent is a contract between society and an inventor. In the interest of spurring innovation, society agrees to protect an inventor's control over an invention. In return, the inventor must publicly disclose the details of the invention. The information made available thus potentially spurs further innovation. A patent protects the implementation of an invention's underlying idea.

Patent Types

There are three types of patents:

Utility patents are granted on what most people think of as an invention—a machine or a process. Utility patents are further broken down into three types: chemical, mechanical, and electrical. Some patents are squeezed into one of these three categories when their placement is not obvious. Computer software, for example, in some instances is patented as a set of instructions to an electrical component, thereby putting the patent into the electrical category. Pharmaceuticals are placed in the chemical category. (The United States is one of the few countries that allows patents on drugs.) Gene splicing techniques and the recently patented Harvard Mouse, a strain of laboratory mouse that has been genetically manipulated to contract cancer readily, fall into the chemical category.

Design patents are granted on the appearance of something. For example, in making a chair with a pedestal instead of four legs, an inventor does not reinvent the chair, but only changes its appearance. The design can be protected, but not the concept of the chair itself.

Plant patents are granted on bushes, trees, roses, and so forth, that are reproduced asexually with human intervention; that is, they do not occur naturally and are not propagated by tubers. A patent rose, for example, is a particular type or color of rose that is protected from duplication by other horticulturalists. Interestingly, because a patented part of a plant is its color, these patents are issued in color booklets rather than in the standard black-and-white patent document. A problem for librarians is that microfilm of plant patents is unavailable because the drawings must be in color.

Requirements for Patenting

There are three requirements for an invention to receive a United States patent:

The invention must be the first of its kind. The patent statutes mention a concept called "anticipation." This means that the invention may not have been disclosed anywhere, by the inventor or anyone else, before an application is submitted. The rationale for this rule is what separates patenting in the United States from patenting in some other industrialized nations. In the United States, only the person who first invents a device has the right to patent it. In some other countries (Japan, for example), the first person to obtain the patent has the right to the invention. To protect the inventor's right to his or her invention, it is necessary to ensure that the idea is an original thought of the inventor by verifying that the idea did not exist before application was made. There must be no other patent like it, not only in the United States, but in the world. Also there must be no mention of the invention in any printed matter, such as a magazine or newspaper, and no evidence that the invention was ever in public use. In one case an invention presented in a single copy of a thesis in Russian that was held by a Chinese library was considered to be public knowledge.

The invention must be useful. This means, as pointed out earlier, that an invention must have a function. This requirement has never been a problem. If an invention is not useful, an inventor is unlikely to expend the time and expense necessary to obtain a patent. Of course, usefulness is sometimes a questionable call. "Rube Goldberg" devices—complicated machines that perform simple tasks—are patentable and useful, but it is probably not worth the time and expense to an inventor to apply for a patent on such devices. (Later in this book there is a discussion of frivolous patents.) The only exception to the concept of usefulness would be in the case of plant patents, where the "invention" is simply attractive and performs no function.

The invention must not be obvious to others of ordinary skill in the field to which the patent pertains. This is the ultimate condition, and it attempts to measure an abstract thing: the technical accomplishment reflected in the invention. For example, substituting one material for another or changing the size is usually not patentable. However, it is up to the examiner to decide which minor changes will and which will not differentiate a new invention from an existing patented invention. This reliance on judgment demonstrates why examiners must have a technical background.

Patent Examiners

The best-educated bureaucrats in Washington, D.C., are at the PTO. Many hold doctorates in their field and have legal training. These are the people who actually look at patent applications to determine if an invention is new, useful, and not obvious. There are about 1,600 patent examiners and 200 trademark examiners.

Patent Pending

Often seen on new products, the term *patent pending* means that a patent application has been submitted. Use of the phrase is simply a marketing technique to give the manufacturer a head start. Because the inventor of the product is first in line for a possible patent, others are discouraged from applying for a patent on the same product. However, the term patent pending offers no protection under the law because an application may be rejected. It is unlawful to mark an item patent pending if an application is not on file. A person may copy and manufacture an invention marked patent pending without fear of litigation until the first-in-line patent is issued. It is unlikely that a person would steal an idea marked patent pending, however, because once a patent is issued, the time and expense the copier spent on manufacture would be lost.

Also, during the application procedure, patent forms are kept secret so that no others may copy the device. Employees of the PTO are prohibited from owning patents to further assure the confidentiality of the process.

Patent Expiration

A patent is good for twenty years from the date of issue; design patents are also valid for twenty years. A patent cannot be renewed or extended except by an act of Congress. After twenty years the patent becomes public property and anyone can copy or manufacture the item. To keep a patent in effect, the inventor pays maintenance fees for those twenty years. The same device cannot be patented again by the original inventor or by another person once a patent has been granted, even though the patent has expired.

How then has a company such as Coca-Cola protected the formula for its soft drink for over a century? The answer is that the formula is not patented; it is a *trade secret* and need not be released publicly. There is more on trade secrets in the trademark section of this book.

Another question librarians are often asked about patent expiration is: If the formula for Tide laundry detergent expired after twenty years and anyone now can copy the formula, how does Tide keep its customers happy if the same detergent is available from other manufacturers at a cheaper price? The answer is that the company comes up with a new, improved Tide, which has an altered chemical formula and is granted a new patent. Who then would want to buy the old, unimproved Tide?

The same concept holds for drug manufacturers. A successful drug such as Valium can make a lot of money for a pharmaceutical company, but after twenty years the company is pressured to develop a new tranquilizer because other drug companies may then manufacture Valium as a generic drug. Generic drugs are available from the pharmacy because the patent has expired.

Patentee and Assignee

A *patentee* is the person who is named as the inventor of the patent. An *assignee* is the person or company to whom the patentee has given rights to the invention. Licensing permits others to use a patent by paying fees to the patentee.

A patentee may license, assign, or sell a patent for a variety of reasons: the inventor may need money immediately, or cannot afford to manufacture the invention on his own, or has no knowledge of marketing techniques. In some cases an employee's contract states that she must assign rights to any patent obtained during the time of her employment to her employer.

The patentee does not have to be a single individual; several people may hold joint rights if they all contributed intellectually to the invention.

"Contributed intellectually" means they were involved in the actual inventing of the device. For example, if an inventor's brother gives $1,000 to finance the development of a widget but has no input into the actual inventing of the widget, the patent cannot be issued in both the inventor's and the brother's names nor can the brother be the assignee unless he has filed forms with the PTO showing that he has purchased rights to the invention. Only the true inventor(s) can obtain a patent.

In many cases, large corporations make the right to become assignees to an employee's patent a condition of employment. Any employee in this situation is legally bound to transfer rights to the employer for any invention related to the company's work that was developed during hours of employment with the company.

After the PTO grants a patent, it usually does not act on an inventor's behalf except in cases of reexaminations or reissues. Any violation of an inventor's patent rights is pursued through the courts and not through the PTO. Many inventors have been ruined economically by fighting infringement cases in the courts. Some patentees attempt to sell their patents if litigation is pending because it then becomes the assignee's responsibility to defend the patent in court.

Assigning and Licensing Patents

A patent is personal property and may be sold, bequeathed in a will, passed to the heirs of a deceased patentee, or licensed. In addition, assigning and licensing are two ways to get an invention marketed and manufactured if the inventor decides not to do this personally.

To assign a patent, an inventor sells the patent to another party; in licensing, an inventor retains ownership of the patent. In selling an invention, the patentee has only to agree on a price with a buyer, file a Certificate of Assignment with the PTO, and pay a nominal fee. The owner of the patent is then the party who bought the patent, and rights to manufacture, distribute, and control the invention belong to the buyer, not to the true inventor. An attorney should handle the agreement because there are several factors to consider. The price should be high enough to reflect the time, effort, and money spent on the idea as well as its earning potential but low enough to realize the risk and development money a buyer would need to invest.

Licensing is a different matter in that the patentee retains ownership of the invention, but allows others to market and manufacture it. Usually an inventor will agree on a percentage of profits when a patent is licensed.

Again, any such agreement is best left to qualified attorneys, not only to handle the agreement but also to advise the inventor on the best course of action. The issues faced by an inventor in licensing an invention are more complex than simply deciding to whom to license it. For example, is the licensee required to produce a certain number of units per year? If not, the licensee may simply purchase the rights and sit on the invention. The patentee then receives only an advance paid when the agreement is signed and does not receive a share of the profits. Does the licensee have exclusive rights, or does the patentee want to license the invention to more than one party? This may be a consideration when one licensee's marketing ability is not national or international or when a licensee markets to only one type of industry. There are other considerations also: the ability to audit the licensee's financial records, the licensee's responsibility in case of infringement, the handling of the invention in case of bankruptcy of either party, and the right to terminate the agreement. As noted earlier, an attorney is best qualified to answer these questions.

Reissued Patents

When patents are issued, the patent document contains many pieces of information: the name(s) of the inventor(s); a brief description of the invention; several drawings of the invention from differing angles, including close-ups of components or subassemblies; "claims," which are the words that explain precisely what is new and unique about this invention; a long description of the invention and sometimes a brief background of the technology or need that necessitated it; and a short list of related patents and classifications searched. On occasion, a patent is issued that contains a mistake in one of these important components. There may be a mistake in the wording of a claim, for example. When this happens the inventor fixes the problems and a new number is assigned. In the lists of patent numbers that a searcher may use, *RE* before the number easily identifies the reissued patents.

Chapter 7

Misconceptions about Patents

In the two hundred years that the patent system has been in use, misconceptions and myths about patents and patenting have established themselves firmly in the minds of the public. Because librarians are confronted with this false information when attempting to help those seeking patent information, it is important that librarians have accurate facts. This chapter has been written with amateur inventors in mind—it is they who are most likely to seek assistance from a librarian. Librarians should also be aware that in explaining the misconceptions held by many amateur inventors or patent searchers, it is easy to discourage their patent research efforts.

REAPING GREAT REWARDS

Patenting an invention does not lead to easy wealth. Most often the opposite is true. Until the twentieth century, the United States was a rural nation without large-scale economic development. Many individuals were self-sufficient, and many were self-educated. Individuals with technical talent in this environment could become rich through the invention of a single, simple device. Today, however, this is rarely the case.

Only 2 to 3 percent of inventions are economically successful. A variety of reasons account for this: An inventor may have no way of producing the invention; the inventor may have overestimated the demand for a new product; the ancillary technology to support extensive consumer use of the invention may not be available (remember Edison, who had to "invent" the electric company in order to sell light bulbs); or the invention may be infringed upon without the true inventor's having the economic resources to pursue court action. The belief that if a person builds a better mousetrap the world will beat a path to her door is a false belief in today's world. More likely the inventor must beat a path to the door of the world—that is, aggressively market and promote the invention. Victor Hugo wrote, "Greater than the tread of mighty armies is an idea whose time has come." That may still be true, but to make the world aware of that idea, it is necessary to bridge the gap between the person with creativity and the person with the capabilities and facilities to market and manufacture the invention.

The biggest problem inventors have is licensing or selling their invention. Although there are many dreamers, creators, and innovators, few of them also have the needed sales skills. As mentioned earlier, many great ideas never are marketed and never make a dime for their inventor. One case of an inventor finding the right marketer at the right time, however, is that of Emma De Sarro.

In the 1950s, Emma De Sarro designed a roller skate with all four wheels in a straight line. Ms. De Sarro spent $900 of her own money developing a prototype and getting patent 3,387,852 for "Detachable and Removable Roller Skates" based on the concept of "single longitudinal wheels mounted on special frames" (see fig. 7.1). When she tried on her own to interest the Chicago Roller Skate Company in buying the patent, she was rejected. In desperation she contacted an invention marketing company that took her money, but provided no marketing services.

In the 1980s, several marketing people became interested in the skates, most notably Mary Horwath. Horwath saw the potential of marketing the in-line skates to urban youths not attracted by traditional roller skating. Using the trade name Roller Blades, Horwath licensed De Sarro's patent and marketed the skates as speedy footwear for hip urban teenagers. The Roller Blade carton was covered with pictures of city graffiti, and the advertising campaign conveyed an image of recklessness and independence. The skates' success has created an industry worth $250 million a year.

WITHHOLDING MANUFACTURE

Many inventors believe that if they invent a product that will cut into the profits of a large corporation, the corporation will buy the patent rights to

FIGURE 7.1

Emma De Sarro's Patent for In-line Roller Skates

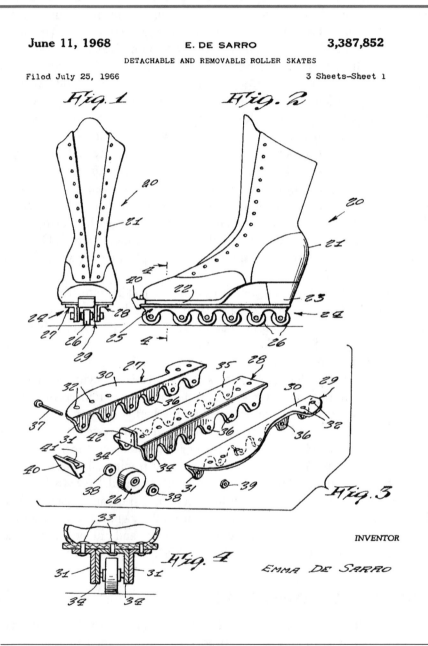

June 11, 1968   E. DE SARRO   3,387,852

DETACHABLE AND REMOVABLE ROLLER SKATES

Filed July 25, 1966   3 Sheets—Sheet 1

Fig. 1   *Fig. 2*

Fig. 3

Fig. 4

INVENTOR

EMMA DE SARRO

keep the new invention off the market. Every five years or so, one particular story goes around about a carburetor that will allow an automobile to achieve over one hundred miles per gallon. In reality, the modern automotive marketplace is so competitive that any advantage would be promoted and accepted as a means of selling more product. Curtailing competition in the worldwide automobile industry is an absurd notion. However, that being said, some companies in other industries do buy or attempt to control the patents of an entire industry in order to stop the manufacture of competing products.

For example, the in-line skating industry is growing rapidly. Patents on new developments in in-line skating have several more years to run, and manufacturers have large inventories of skates based on these existing patents. If a new, improved in-line skate is patented, it is in the best interest of a company to purchase the patent and sit on it until the inventories of older skates are depleted. If a single manufacturer can control all the new developments in a particular industry, it can effectively control the industry and stifle competition.

A patent search, explained in later chapters, often reveals that the unique idea that would lead to riches is already patented. One amateur inventor spent over $1,000 on drawings, specifications, and a market study of a water shutoff system before deciding to do a patent search for any similar devices. This inventor's idea was to place a valve and a solenoid on the water supply line to a house. The configuration was such that if the water pipe suddenly burst from freezing or some other break in the line, the measured increase in water flow would trip the solenoid and close the valve, preventing water damage to the house. The flash of inspiration came to this inventor when the hose on his washing machine burst and flooded his entire house while he was away. A simple patent search that took only one day revealed that such a device had already been patented by a person who lived in Leadville, Colorado (a very cold place in the winter). The device was never successful because a valid market study revealed that water pipes do not burst often, except for the water line attached to a washing machine. Simply turning off the supply valve to the washer until laundry day or purchasing a hose enmeshed in a stainless steel fabric easily solves the problem. Consumers felt the risk wasn't worth the expense of installing a shutoff device on a main water line.

OBTAINING AN INTERNATIONAL PATENT

Librarians should be aware that an inventor cannot obtain an international or "world" patent. A U.S. patent is not enforceable outside the United States and a foreign patent is not enforceable in the United States. Protection is acquired by filing an application in each country in which protection is desired—an expensive and time-consuming procedure.

An alternative approach is to file an International Application under the Patent Cooperation Treaty (PCT). Again, it must be stressed that this does not provide an international patent, but minimizes the cost and procedures resulting from international patent filings. The PCT, signed in 1970, has forty-five participating countries and allows a patentee to file a single application. This application then has to be filed with each national patent office. The advantage is that a single application may be copied and then submitted in each PCT country rather than having to produce a separate application for each country.

Under the PCT, an international patent search is carried out by one of the major patent offices, resulting in a report that lists documents in any PCT participating country that may affect the patentability of the invention in a particular country. On the negative side, once the application is filed there is little saving of time or expense as the inventor goes through each nation's patent procedure. Another negative aspect is that because so many countries and patents are involved in the search, there is a greater chance for error than in a country-by-country search.

Other treaties also govern international patents. For example, the World Intellectual Property Organization (WIPO) governs the Paris Convention. The Paris Convention, signed by eleven countries in 1883 and now signed by one hundred countries, including the United States, has proved to be one of the most enduring and successful acts of international cooperation ever created. Although revised several times, the basic concept of the Paris Convention remains the same. An inventor who files for patent protection in any of the participating countries has twelve months to apply for protection in any of the other countries. These other applications are considered to have been filed on the same day as the original application. That is, only the original inventor may file an application in any Paris Convention country for one year. Other applications, even if filed earlier in a participating country, are considered secondary to the original application.

The great advantage is that an application does not have to be filed in all countries at the same time. An inventor has a year to decide in which countries she or he may desire protection and to estimate the expense of preparing applications for those countries. Despite its having endured for over one hundred years, the Paris Convention is now under attack by third world countries. These countries are appealing to GATT, the General Agreement on Tariffs and Trade, to make sweeping changes in the Paris Convention to provide open markets and free trade based on fair competition. These third world countries regard patents as constituting unfair competition, especially in the area of pharmaceuticals. In most of the developed world, pharmaceuticals are not patented because their distribution serves the good of all humankind, but some countries, such as India, see the ability to monopolize medicines as basic to their economic development. (The United States is one of the few countries that allow patents on pharmaceuticals.)

WIPO does more than serve as administrator for the Paris Convention. WIPO administers seventeen separate intellectual property agreements worldwide, but its biggest contribution is in the creation of an international patent classification system.

PRODUCING A MODEL

One recurring image about patents comes from cartoons that show a person sitting outside a patent office door with a model of a ridiculous invention. The requirement of a model with each patent application was dropped in 1870, although for about a decade thereafter the PTO called for them frequently. The PTO still has a right to call for a model if necessary to prove operability, but seldom asks for one. In a recent application for a perpetual motion machine, the PTO required a working model. Normally, the PTO will return the application and fees to anyone attempting to patent a perpetual motion machine.

The reasons for dropping the model requirement are straightforward. First, there would be no practical way to store the 70,000 models that would be submitted each year. Second, as technology becomes more complicated, the expense of building, say, a working space station is impractical. Third, because examiners are engineers, they are able to determine an invention's workability from the drawings and do not need to rely on a working model. Finally, patent drawings are made according to exact specifications to reveal the working nature of an invention. An experienced draftsman cannot simply draw up some blueprints for an inventor. The draftsman must be a registered patent draftsman and follow PTO guidelines exactly, including different types of shading to designate colors and a specific method of labeling components in the drawing.

CLOSING THE PTO

The one myth that will not go away is that in the nineteenth century a patent commissioner wanted to close the PTO because he felt that everything had already been invented. In reality, during the John Quincy Adams administration (1825–1829), Congress came within three votes of discontinuing the Patent and Trademark Office. The vote, however, was not made because it was felt that everything had been invented. Congress felt that registering ideas was simply a bureaucratic routine. At the time, the Patent Office was hardly overrun with patent applications; patent numbering would not begin for another decade. Congress was just hoping to save the taxpayers money. Another source of this legend is a paragraph in the 1843 annual report of the commissioner of patents, Henry L. Ellsworth: "The advancement of the arts, from year to year, taxes our credulity and seems to presage the arrival of that period when human improvement must end." The commissioner had simply added a rhetorical flourish, common in the writing of the day, to emphasize the rapid progress of inventions at that time and did not mean to suggest that everything had been invented, but, rather, that in some future paradise everything would exist.

PATENTING BY AMATEURS

Amateur inventors are often lured by late-night television commercials in which private companies promise to assist them in obtaining a patent and in producing a market study. The cost of such services, usually several hundred dollars, is much greater than an initial consultation with a patent attorney. Many registered patent attorneys will offer an initial consultation at no charge to evaluate the viability of an inventor's idea. The "market study" is sometimes a simple list of potential manufacturers taken from the *Thomas Register.* Of course, some of these businesses are reputable, but inventors should exercise caution in dealing with any of them. A reputable company would not charge exorbitant fees for services that may be obtained cheaper elsewhere (for example, a list of manufacturers), nor would a reputable company try to dissuade a person from seeking outside legal counsel. As always in patent matters, an inventor should have legal representation first before agreeing to speak with any company or signing anything.

One amateur inventor had been very successful in making fabric head guards for livestock. She would buy material and sew the pieces together in her home, then take the completed products to local feed and livestock stores and sell them on consignment. The head guards, which kept insects from biting the livestock, sold well because they were made of a lightweight mesh, had easily adjustable Velcro straps, and were able to fit a variety of animals from horses to cows. They were unlike anything then on the market.

One store owner suggested that the inventor patent the design of her head guard so that others would not copy it and destroy her growing business. When she attempted to perform a patent search at a local patent depository library, she revealed to the librarian that she had been making the head guards for three years before deciding to get a patent. As explained in chapter 1, this would invalidate a patent application because of the concept of anticipation.

FRIVOLOUS AND UNUSUAL PATENTS

In chapter 1, mention was made of a patent application for a method of keeping a severed human head alive. This was a practical joke, and a patent was never issued on the process. There are, however, throughout the patent classification system, patents that are humorous, strange, unorthodox, or frivolous. The reasons for these patents' existence are as varied as the patents themselves. Some inventors are sincere in their belief that they have really invented a better mousetrap; some patents may simply be an exercise in self-promotion or are the quintessential stroke of an iconoclast. Some of the inventions presented here are unusual not because the patent is unusual, but because the inventor is.

Many people, famous in entertainment, politics, or other fields, have ventured into patenting. Only one president, Abraham Lincoln, was granted a patent. His method for "Buoying Vessels over Shoals," patent 6,469, was granted in 1849—before he was elected president. The invention used air chambers to lift steamships over shallow water or shoals (see fig. 7.2). Thomas Jefferson, the third president and first patent commissioner, was the most prolific presidential inventor although he never obtained patents on his inventions. Jefferson invented the pedometer and a hemp-treating machine, among other things.

The beverage blender is a relatively old machine, invented in 1922 by J. Poplawski to make his favorite drink, the milkshake. In the 1930s Fred Waring, director of a choral group called The Pennsylvanians, invented an

FIGURE 7.2

Lincoln Patent Letter (Partial)

UNITED STATES PATENT OFFICE

ABRAHAM LINCOLN, OF SPRINGFIELD, ILLINOIS.

BUOYING VESSELS OVER SHOALS.

Specification forming part of Letters Patent No. 6,469, dated May 22, 1849; application filed
March 10, 1849.

To all whom it may concern:

Be it known that I, Abraham Lincoln, of Springfield, in the County of Sangamon, in the State of Illinois, have invented a new and improved manner of combining adjustable buoyant air chambers with a steamboat or other vessel for the purpose of enabling their draught of water to be readily lessened to enable them to pass over bars, or through shallow water, without discharging their cargoes; and I do hereby declare the following to be a full, clear, and exact description thereof, reference being had to the accompanying drawings making a part of this specification. Similar letters indicate like parts in all the figures.

The buoyant chambers A, A, which I employ, are constructed in such a manner that they can be expanded so as to hold a large volume of air when required for use, and can be contracted, into a very small space and safely secured as soon as their services can be dispensed with.

Fig. 1, is a side elevation of a vessel with the buoyant chambers combined therewith, expanded;

Fig. 2, is a transverse section of the same with the buoyant chambers contracted.

Fig. 3, is a longitudinal vertical section through the centre of one of the buoyant chambers, and the box B, for receiving it when contracted, which is secured to the lower guard of the vessel.

The top g, and bottom h, of each buoyant chamber, is composed of plank or metal, of suitable strength and stiffness, and the flexible sides and ends of the chambers, are composed of india-rubber cloth, or other suitable water-proof fabric, securely united to the edges and ends of the top and bottom of the chambers.

The sides of the chambers may be stayed and supported centrally by a frame k, as shown in Fig. 3, or as many stays may be combined with them as may be necessary to give them the requisite fullness and strength when expanded.

The buoyant chambers are suspended and operated as follows: A suitable number of vertical shafts or spars D, D, are combined with each of the chambers, as represented in Figs. 2 and 3, to wit: The shafts work freely in apertures formed in the upper sides of the chambers, and their lower ends are permanently secured to the under sides of the chambers: The vertical shafts or spars (D,D,) pass up through the top of the boxes B, B, on the lower guards of the vessel, and then through its upper guards, or some other suitable support, to keep them in a vertical position.

The vertical shafts (D, D,) are connected to the main shaft C, which passes longitudinally through the centre of the vessel—just below its upper deck—by endless ropes f, f, as represented in Fig. 2: The said ropes, f, f, being wound several times around the main shaft C, then passing outwards over sheaves or rollers attached to the upper deck or guards of the vessel, from which they descend over the inner sides of the vertical shafts or spars D, D, to sheaves or rollers connected to the boxes B, B, and thence rise to the main shaft (C,) again.

The ropes f, f, are connected to the vertical shafts at i, i, as shown in Figs. 1 and 2. It will therefore be perceived, that by turning the main shaft C, in one direction, the buoyant chambers will be expanded into the position shown in Fig. 1; and by turning the shaft in an opposite direction, the chambers will be contracted into the position shown in Fig. 2.

In Fig. 3, e, e, are check ropes, made fast to the tops of the boxes B, B, and to the upper sides of the buoyant chambers; which ropes catch and retain the upper sides of the chambers when their lower sides are forced down, and cause the chambers to be expanded to their full capacity. By varying the length of the check ropes, the depth of immersion of the buoyant chambers can be governed. A suitable number of openings m, m, are formed in the upper sides of the buoyant chambers, for the admission and emission of air when the chambers are expanded and contracted.

The ropes f, f, that connect the main shaft C, with the shafts or spars D, D, (rising from improved portable blender to make his favorite drink, the daiquiri. Waring was a Penn State architectural and engineering student in his youth and was known by his friends to spend time tinkering with gadgets. With Frederick Osius, Waring came up with the idea of a portable machine to mix liquids. The Waring Blender was a huge success.

Actress Hedy Lamarr gained fame in films in the 1930s and 1940s. Although she always played the siren and dependent female, few knew that in real life she possessed a first-rate intellect. In 1941, under the name Hedy Kaiser Markey, she was granted patent 2,292,387 on a secret radio system for torpedoes (see fig. 7.3). Enemies could detect the remote control guidance systems of torpedoes because they could monitor the radio frequency coming from the torpedoes' controllers. In Lamarr's patent, the radio frequency changed continually and was kept track of by means of a paper punch tape, allowing the sender to guide the torpedo to its target without its being detected by the enemy.

Other famous people have tried their hand at patenting. Albert Einstein invented a means of refrigeration using butane and ammonia (see fig. 7.4). Edgar Bergen holds patent D129,255 on a ventriloquist's dummy (see fig. 7.5). Zeppo Marx, one of the famous Marx Brothers comedy team, was granted patent 3,426,747 on a watch driven by a pulse rate. Walt Disney patented his famous Mad Hatter's Teacup Ride in 1957 (see fig. 7.6). Mark Twain invented a trivia game in 1885 (patent 324,535) that was a dismal failure. Always most interesting, however, are the unknown inventors who patent outrageous devices.

Design patent 270,936, granted to Randall Everson, is for a combined toilet tank and aquarium (see fig. 1.1 in chap. 1). Toilet improvements are highly popular among inventors. Patent 3,477,070 is for a toilet seat lock, practical if there are small children in the house, and patent 3,593,345 is for a toilet seat with an acoustical liner to prevent sounds from being heard by others.

Snoring seems to be a problem addressed by inventors continually. As early as 1897, patent 587,350 was granted on a device that disrupted airflow as it passes into an open mouth. The slotted device was worn in the mouth during sleep and was held in place by an elastic band. As technology marched on, an electronic snore depressor was granted patent 3,480,010 in 1969.

Some patents that seem frivolous are later found to be quite practical. Patent 3,423,150 was for a pair of eyeglasses with tiny, adjustable rearview mirrors (see fig. 7.7). The device was found to be very practical for bicycle riders. Following is a list of other unusual patents. The D in front of a number designates the invention as a design patent. Other unusual and humorous patents can be found at www.colitz.com/site/wacky.htm, www.patent.free-serve.co.uk/, or inventors.about.com/.

D216,807 Nixon statuette

D268,200 Toy space vehicle, a replica of a spaceship used in the Star Wars films; patented by Lucas film

D270,741 game board for Trivial Pursuit

D278,380 Beard bib

D281,720 Tongue cleaner

18,691 Life preserver for a horse

353,197 Chin rest for a smoker's pipe

383,010 device that churns butter while the user swings

395,515 Chewing gum locket (an obvious improvement over the bedpost)

556,248 Self-tipping hat to assure proper manners even when the wearer's hands are full

586,025 Combined grocer's package, grater, slicer, mousetrap, and fly trap

968,325 Kick-me game

1,370,316 Harry Houdini's diving suit

3,335; 81,497; 500,072; 901,407; 1,436,757 Devices allowing escape from a buried coffin

2,636,176 Coat for two

3,211,132 Training pants for dogs

3,589,009 Electric spaghetti fork

3,823,494 Shoe that leaves a backward footprint

4,044,405 Target for a urinal

4,502,243 Insect hammer

4,541,726 Twenty-five-hour clock

FIGURE 7.3

Hedy Lamarr's Patent for a Torpedo Guidance System

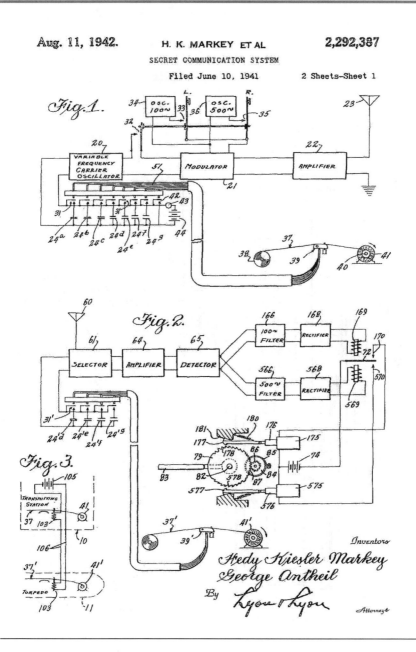

FIGURE 7.4

Einstein's Patent for a Refrigeration Method

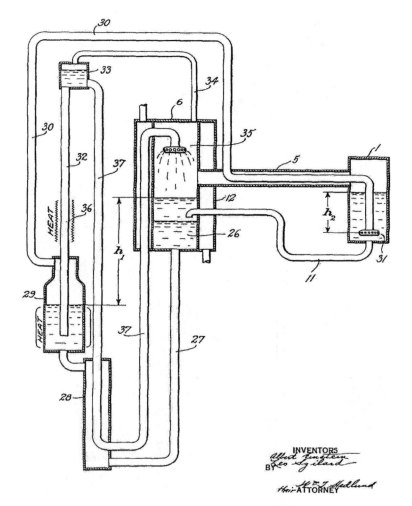

Nov. 11, 1930.   A. EINSTEIN ET AL   1,781,541
                                    REFRIGERATION
                              Filed Dec. 16, 1927

FIGURE 7.5

Edgar Bergen's Patent for a Ventriloquist's Dummy

Sept. 2, 1941.   E. BERGEN   Des. 129,255

DOLL HEAD OR SIMILAR ARTICLE

Filed Oct. 26, 1940

INVENTOR

Edgar Bergen

BY Kenyon & Kenyon

ATTORNEYS

FIGURE 7.6

Walt Disney's Patent for Teacup Ride

United States Patent Office

Des. 180,585
Patented July 9, 1957

180,585

PASSENGER CARRYING AMUSEMENT DEVICE

Walter E. Disney, Los Angeles, Calif., assignor to Disney-
land, Inc., Anaheim, Calif., a corporation of California

Application July 17, 1956, Serial No. 42,274

Term of patent 14 years

(Cl. D34—5)

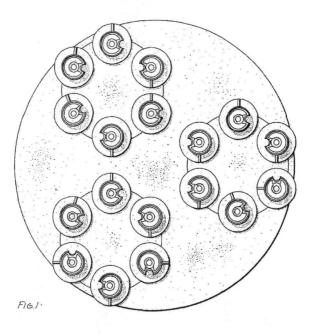

FIG.1·

FIG.2

FIGURE 7.7

J. A. Freed's Patent for Eyeglasses with Rearview Mirrors

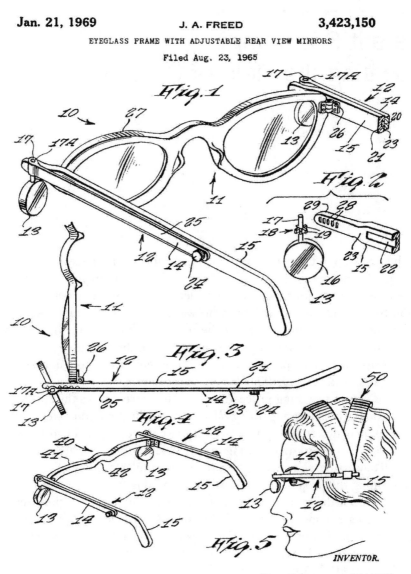

Jan. 21, 1969   J. A. FREED   3,423,150

EYEGLASS FRAME WITH ADJUSTABLE REAR VIEW MIRRORS

Filed Aug. 23, 1965

INVENTOR.

JOSEPH A. FREED

Chapter 8

Patent Searching: Locating the Field of Search

The first step in the patent process is to perform a patent search to assure that the invention does not already exist. Librarians in government document depository libraries and patent depository libraries often are called upon to assist amateur inventors who want to search a patent themselves before deciding whether to invest the money to hire an attorney. Unique problems arise when assisting amateur patent searchers. One obstacle is the complexity of the U.S. patent classification system, which contains over 400 major classifications and 108,000 subclassifications.

The patent searching procedure presented here divides the search into two major areas: locating the *field of search* (the first four steps of the process), and determining *prior art* (the last three steps). Field of search assists the searcher in determining in what "field" or subject area a patent is most likely to be classified. The process is similar to that of a librarian determining the proper subject heading for a book.

Prior art is the process of viewing the "prior" or previously patented art. *Art* to the Patent and Trademark Office means any invention. Prior art thus guides the searcher in locating existing patents in a related subject area that may be similar to the invention being searched. Prior art is somewhat like viewing a MARC record screen to determine if the information displayed accurately describes the book a cataloger has in hand.

The seven-step procedure explained here is a quick-start method that can be used by librarians to assist amateurs through the often-rocky terrain of patent searching. Searchers or librarians need not read the entire seven steps before proceeding, but may perform each step as they come to it. Following the steps in order ensures that the patent search proceeds rapidly and eliminates unnecessary legal and technical explanations that often confuse inexperienced searchers.

STEP 1
Identify the Parts of the Invention

Even if all the technology and online resources in the world are available to a patent searcher, this first step is still an intellectual process best carried out with a pen and paper. A necessary part of a patent search involves identifying and listing an invention's major components. A component is a device that by itself could be patented. Usually a patent is a combination of several small inventions working together. It is rare today to find an invention that consists of only one device or that can be described with only one term; however, if an invention has only one application, that application becomes a word that must be searched in the same way as a component.

For example, a complicated invention such as a bicycle would be identified not only by the term bicycle, but also by the components that may play a role in the functioning of the device—wheel, brake, handle bar, pedal, and so on. If the invention is a bicycle headlight that is powered by a generator, the major components would be: bicycle, light, generator. The bicycle is the major application of the invention; *light* and *generator* are the terms for the components that may be part of a headlight powered by the wheel of a bicycle. Terms for components are aids to help a searcher find the synonyms for the invention being searched.

Often a searcher's thinking is too narrowly focused on the invention being searched. If a searcher were looking for the patents on flying disks, only the trademark Frisbee comes to mind, but more terms for the components that make up the invention can be identified if the searcher is aware of the technology that makes the disk fly. The edge of the disk is shaped like an airplane wing, so the terms *wing* and *airplane* should be included in the list. Generally, the item may be described as a toy, so this becomes a searchable term also.

Occasionally an invention is so simple that no matter how the searcher tries to describe its components, only one or two words come to mind. Indeed some simple inventions have no common name. An example is the

Topsy Tail—a simple hoop on a handle that is used to style long hair after the hair is in a ponytail. Other than the trademarked name Topsy Tail, how would this invention be described? If this happens, the searcher should think of broad synonyms that may be used to describe the invention. In this example, the term hair comes to mind and should be included in a list of component terms to search, although the Topsy Tail is not made of hair and hair plays no role in the invention itself except to describe its application. Other terms may be *comb* and *barrette*, not because they are components of the invention but because their relationship to the application—hair styling—may lead the searcher toward a classification that may include all types of devices to be used in hair styling.

These terms that a searcher thinks of in describing the components of an invention are called *keywords*. These are *not* the keywords librarians are accustomed to, such as a significant word from a title or abstract. Rather, they are closer to subject headings and subheadings that are used in an online catalog. It is important that a searcher be armed with as many keywords as possible before proceeding, even if the words are only marginally related to the invention being searched. The keywords are then searched in the *Index to the U.S. Patent Classification.*

STEP 2
Consult the *Index to the U.S. Patent Classification*

Most government documents depository libraries and all patent depository libraries hold the annual, *Index to the U.S. Patent Classification.* This index is used to locate the patent subject areas, called *classifications,* that categorize an invention. The searcher must have these classifications before proceeding with a patent search.

This search will utilize the patent searching tools available at www.uspto.gov. These tools are also available in a paper format, but the PTO has done such a good job of making them available on the Web that online searching is the preferred method. To get to the index go to www.uspto.gov (see fig. 8.1). This is the home page for the United States Patent and Trademark Office. Click on the bar on the left marked Patents. This is a link to the patent services and resources of the PTO. The resulting page is shown in figure 8.2.

On the patent services page, shown in figure 8.2, in the left-hand column (titled Services), click on the Search Patents link. The resulting page,

FIGURE 8.1
PTO Home Page

FIGURE 8.2
PTO Services and Resources

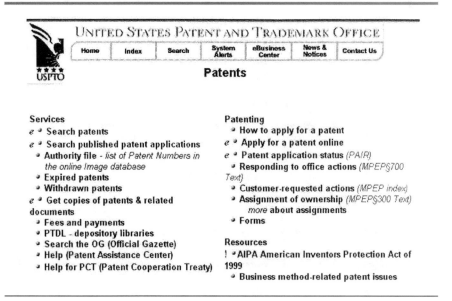

titled Patent Full-Text and Full-Page Image Databases, is shown in figure
8.3. This page is used again farther on in the search process, but at this
point, all the searcher needs is the index. It can be found by clicking on the
link at the bottom of the box—Tools to Help in Searching by Patent
Classification. The resulting page, shown in figure 8.4. is actually the beginning of the manual of classification and lists all patent classes. The searcher
will return to this page in step 3, so it is a good idea to bookmark it. Now,
at the top of the page in figure 8.4, click on the link titled USPC Index. The
resulting page is shown in figure 8.5.

This is the introductory page of the index to classification and contains
an alphabetic list across the bottom of the screen. The patent system is continually changing, and an inaccurate classification found at this step can
lead to a wild goose chase that will be both frustrating and time-consuming. Using the online version of the index assures that the information
found is current. If a searcher uses a paper index, some of the information
may be out of date because the paper version is published only once a year
in December.

A cautionary note for patent searchers using the USPTO website is
appropriate at this point. Librarians and educators who use the World Wide

FIGURE 8.3
Patent Databases

Patent Full-Text and Full-Page Image Databases

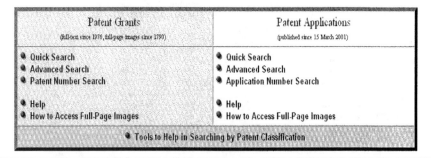

Patent Grants	Patent Applications
(full-text since 1976, full-page images since 1790)	(published since 15 March 2001)
● Quick Search	● Quick Search
● Advanced Search	● Advanced Search
● Patent Number Search	● Application Number Search
● Help	● Help
● How to Access Full-Page Images	● How to Access Full-Page Images
● Tools to Help in Searching by Patent Classification	

FIGURE 8.4

Introductory Page of the Manual of U.S. Patent Classification

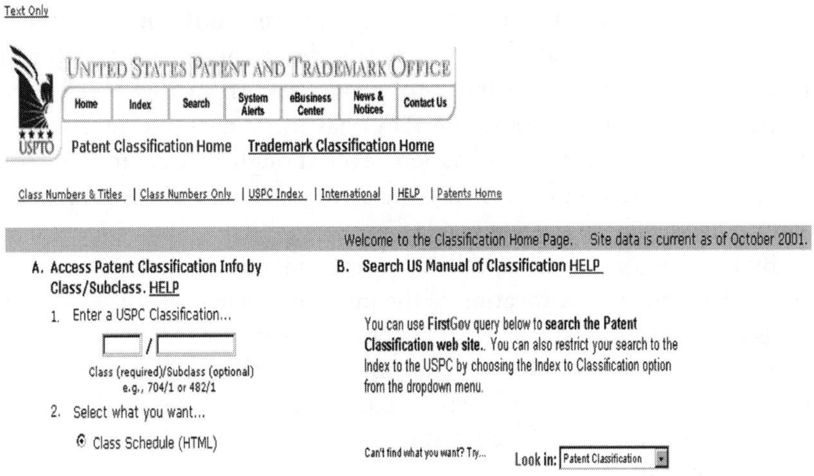

FIGURE 8.5

Introductory Page of the Index to the U.S. Patent Classification

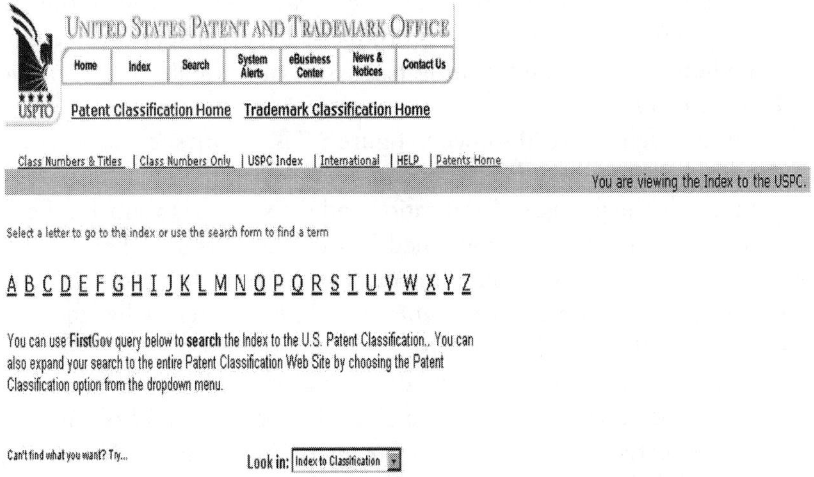

Web are aware that web pages are not static things. These virtual sources of information are updated, revised, and changed in appearance continually. Although every effort has been made to reproduce exact copies of the web pages relating to patent searching, these pages may differ in appearance or contain revised information from what is shown here. If the web page a given reader is viewing is similar to what is shown in this book, but not exactly the same, it is because the PTO has made changes since this book has been published. On a positive note, even though changes may have been made, the information is normally the same, although the appearance and some terms may have been revised.

By looking up the terms, called *keywords*, identified in step 1, a searcher can find the proper classification of the invention being searched. The index contains keywords arranged in alphabetical order.

For clarification of this step, an invention called a "fly mask" will be used. A fly mask is a piece of cloth, usually canvas, that covers the head of a horse or a cow and lets the animal eat and see while being protected from flies (see fig. 8.6).

In step 1, a searcher would have broken down this device into its parts and listed any synonyms that might also describe the device. The components/synonyms would be: *mask, face covering, flies, horse, cow, insects, canvas,* and *livestock.* The goal is to look under as many synonyms and related words as possible to obtain the most access points to the index. It is better to have too many terms than to not have enough because some terms will not appear in the index.

To begin this part of the search process, click the letter *M* in the alphabet displayed (see fig. 8.5). This will produce a list of all keywords beginning with the letter *M*. On the resulting page, shown in figure 8.7, scroll down to the keyword *mask.*

Beneath each keyword shown in figure 8.7 is a more specific description. To the right of these words are two numbers separated by a slash (/). The first number is the primary classification and the second is a subclassification.

A lot of information is contained in this short listing. The "See Face Guards" reference in parentheses means that there is a separate listing in the index alphabetically under *face guards.* The indented terms list the various types of masks that are classified in the system.

The invention being searched, a fly mask, is not listed here, but this is not a dead end. The "see" reference gives the searcher another category to search. The searcher would refer to *face guards* in the index. To do this, go back to the alphabetic listing shown in figure 8.5 and click on *F* for *face guards.*

FIGURE 8.6

Patent for Face Fly Mask

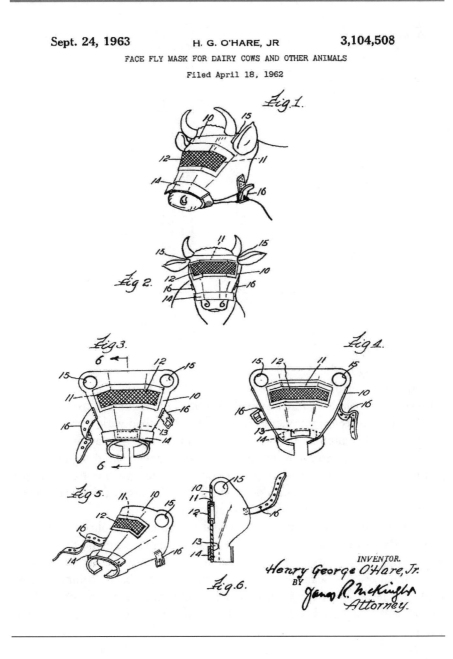

Sept. 24, 1963   H. G. O'HARE, JR   3,104,508

FACE FLY MASK FOR DAIRY COWS AND OTHER ANIMALS

Filed April 18, 1962

FIGURE 8.7

Keywords List

```
Masher ..................................... 241 / 169.2
Mashing ................................... 435 / 93
    Apparatus ............................. 435 / 291.1+
    Beverage preparation .................. 426 / 11
    Kitchen hand tool ..................... D07 / 682
Mask (See  Face Guards)
    Baseball .............................. 2 / 9
    False faces ........................... 2 / 206
    Fire fighting ......................... D29 / 108+
    Gas mask .............................. 425 / 815*
    Head covering with .................... 2 / 173
    Photographic .......................... 430 / 5
    Respirators ........................... 128 / 206.12+
    Surgical or oxygen .................... D24 / 110.1+
    Swimming .............................. D24 / 110.2+
Masking
    Abrading .............................. 451 / 29+
    Coating ............................... 427 / 259
    Dyeing ................................ 8 / 445+
    Electrolysis combined ................. 205 / 118+
    Tape .................................. 428 / 343+
        Making by coating ................. 427 / 207.1+
```

The Symbols

Before looking farther the searcher should learn the meanings of the symbols that accompany the numbers in the column to the left in figure 8.7. Knowing each symbol's function will save time and make the process easier.

Patent classes are numbered rather than described with words. The D in front of a class number means that this patent is a design patent (see chapter 6 for an explanation of utility patents, plant patents, and design patents). If the searcher is not seeking protection for a design, but for a unique device, the classifications preceded by a D may be disregarded even if the words describing the class seem to be appropriate.

The classification numbers displayed may include a plus sign (+), an asterisk (*), or decimal numbers to the right. The plus sign and the asterisk will be explained in step 3 as the searcher learns about the organization of the manual of classification, but the decimals in the subclass column can be explained here. Their origin gives some insight into the history of the U.S. Patent and Trademark Office and the problems of organizing 6 million patents.

The History of Classification

The patent classification system was developed in the nineteenth century. Originally, classes were simply numbered 1, 2, 3, and so on. That part of the classification remains unchanged, and today there are over four hundred class numbers. If new major classifications are needed, they are simply added at the end. However, subclass numbers within each classification are arranged by technology. For example, machinery that operates on electricity will always be subclassed between subclasses 10 and 15 in a particular classification. A problem arose as new technologies were developed. When a totally new group of electrical inventions came along that necessitated their own classification, subclasses 10 through 15 were already being used. Numbers could not simply be added at the end of the subclass because the arrangement was by technology. That is, electric patents had to fit somewhere between 10 and 15 unless the PTO rearranged the entire patent classification system.

The solution was to add a suffix to the subclass number. New electric technologies would be classified as 10A, for example. That worked fine until the PTO ran out of alphabet. Then two-letter prefixes like 10AA or 10AB were used. As more and more patents were added, the classification scheme got so complicated it was possible that a subclass might eventually need to be followed by twenty-six letters. The final solution was to add subclassifications with a decimal, such as 10.1 or 10.22. The decimal solution is used today, and each number represents a unique subclassification. There is a residual problem, however. The PTO never retrospectively changed all the old 10A, 10AB numbers, so a searcher will find a mixture of systems in locating subclassification numbers. Each subclass number, whether it is 10.1, 10A, or 10AB, represents a unique subclass, just as if it were numbered 1, 2, or 3.

Returning to the Search

Because looking under *mask* in the index proved fruitless, the searcher should use the "see" reference and look in the index under *face guards*. This is done by clicking on the letter *F* on the introductory page (see figure 8.6). The resulting page is shown in figure 8.8. However, there is no listing for *face guards*. The correct listing is *face*, and *guards* is listed as a subheading. In addition, *guards* refers the searcher back to *masks*, but there is no listing for *masks*—the correct listing, as the searcher is already aware, is the singular *mask*.

This may seem like nit-picking, but this example brings up an important point about the editorial control throughout the entire range of tools that are used in performing a patent search. There are many spelling errors, capitalization errors, incorrect references, and downright mistakes! The system is designed for legal professionals, who come to the search with a certain amount of background knowledge, but amateur searchers are often thrown off the track and frustrated by not finding information where they have been told they can find it. Searchers should be careful of this and do not assume that what is printed literally in the patent tools must be correct. Many times it isn't.

Listed under *guards*, as a further subcategory, is "animal restraining type." This may look tantalizing because it mentions animals, but do not be misled. A fly mask is not used for restraining an animal. *Face guards* and *mask*

FIGURE 8.8

Keywords List

510 / 515	+ - - - - . . FOR LAUNDRY USE
	- - - - FACE
602 / 74	+ - - - - . . BANDAGE
433 / 73	- - - - . . BOWS DENTAL
433 / 5	- - - - . . . . . ORTHODONTIC
002 / 206	- - - - . . COVERINGS
607 / 139	+ - - - - . . . . . WITH THERAPUETIC MEANS
002 / 206	- - - - . . FALSE
002 / 173	- - - - . . . . . HAT COMBINED
002 / 9	- - - - . . GUARDS (SEE MASKS)
119 / 821	+ - - - - . . . . . ANIMAL RESTRAINING TYPE
602 / 17	- - - - . . LIFTER ORTHOPEDIC
	- - - - . . MILL CUTTER
409 / 10	+ - - - - . . . . . GEAR GENERATING
409 / 64	+ - - - - : . . . . ROTARY
	- - - - . . PLATES
174 / 55	+ - - - - . . . . . ELECTRICAL BOX
174 / 66	+ - - - - . . . . . ELECTRICAL BOX
070 / 450	- - - - . . . . . LOCKS
250 / 466.1	. - - - - . . . . . LUMINOUS
220 / 241	- - - - . . . . . RECEPTACLE CLOSURE
105 / 21	+ - - - - . . . . . TRAIN VESTIBULE
105 / 10	+ - - - - . . . . . TRAIN VESTIBULE EXPANDERS FOR

are now a dead end, but recall in step 1 the searcher described the invention with many terms—*mask, face covering, flies,* and so on. The searcher should now try the next term in the list, *flies,* by going back to the alphabetic listing in figure 8.6, clicking again on the letter *F,* and scrolling down to *fly.* The resulting page is shown in figure 8.9.

It may seem a little silly to be looking under *flies* because insects are not considered inventions. The rational person would disregard this approach, but the searcher should track down every clue. In figure 8.9, the index is reproduced for the term *fly.* Although *flies* is not listed, *fly* is. Be aware of this—words listed in the index may have more than one meaning. That is, a fly is an insect, but to the PTO a fly is also something used by fishermen, the zipper on trousers, the opening in a shoe that holds the laces, or any of dozens of other things. Although the classification scheme itself is organized as to type of technology, the index is not. It is a true keyword listing without regard to definition.

FIGURE 8.9

Keywords List

324 / 244	+ - - - - ..	MAGNETIC FLUX
	- - - -	**FLY**
416 / 501	* - - - - ..	BRUSH
012 / 113	- - - - ..	CLOSER LASTING TOOL
043 / 42.24	+ . - - - - ..	FISHING
D22 / 125	+ - - - -	DESIGN
043 / 57.1	+ . - - - -	HOLDERS FOR FISHHOOKS, FLIES
054 / 80.4	. - - - - ..	NET
493 / 52	+ - - - - ..	PAPER BOX MAKING
043 / 137	- - - - ..	SWATTER
D22 / 124	- - - -	DESIGN
057 / 96	- - - - ..	TEXTILE SPINNING
043 / 122	- - - - ..	TRAP
106 / DIG 1	- - - -	**FLY ASH**
264 / DIG 49	- - - - ..	PROCESSES OF USING
428 / 406	- - - - ..	STOCK MATERIAL
	- - - -	**FLYING (SEE AIRCRAFT)**
	- - - - ..	BLIND
244 / 75R	+ - - - -	AIRCRAFT CONTROLS
340 / 947	+ - - - -	TRAFFIC CONTROL SYSTEMS
D21 / 443	+ - - - - ..	DISC (DESIGN)
244	- - - - ..	MACHINE

Look down the list of subheadings under *fly*. No fly mask or face guard is listed, but as was pointed out earlier, the searcher should not assume that a common term for a device is the term that the PTO will use. There is a clue here that an experienced patent searcher would see right away. An amateur searcher, however, might meet with another dead end. The clue will be revealed later in this step.

The next term that was listed in step 1 is *horse*. Figure 8.10 shows the listing from the index. Still no fly mask or anything related to it appears, but there are clues here. The amateur searcher who is also the inventor of the device might discover the clues because the inventor would know something about livestock apparatus. What broad category of horse tack would a fly mask fit into? Also, notice the column of subclass numbers in figure 8.10. Something is missing.

FIGURE 8.10

Keywords List

```
368 / 62      + - - - - .. WATCHES
              - - - - HORSE
054 / 79.1    . - - - - .. BLANKETS
D30 / 145     - - - - ..... DESIGN
054 / 82      - - - - .. BOOTS
D30 / 146     + - - - - ..... DESIGN
054 / 19.1    + . - - - - .. COLLARS
D30 / 137     - - - - ..... DESIGN
054 / 18.1    + . - - - - ..... HAMES COMBINED
069 / 3       - - - - ..... SHAPING
069 / 4       - - - - ..... STUFFING
119 / 436     + - - - - .. CONFINING AND HOUSING
278 / 21      + - - - - .. DETACHERS
182 / 181.1   + . - - - - .. FOUR LEGGED SUPPORT
182 / 153     + - - - - ..... UNITARY FOLDABLE
119 / 600     + - - - - .. GROOMING AND CURRYING DEVICES
015 / 363     + - - - - ..... WITH AIR DRAFT
482 / 25      - - - - .. GYMNASTIC
054           - - - - .. HARNESS
185 / 15      + - - - - .. POWERED MOTOR
185 / 3       - - - - ..... : COMPOSITE OR MULTIPLE
056 / 375     + - - - - .. RAKE HORSE DRAWN
```

The subclass number for Harness is missing; only the class number is given—class 54. This happens often in the index, purposely and not because of poor editorial control. It means that all types of horse harness may be found in class 54, but a specific item must be further defined to locate its subclass. In figures 8.8 and 8.9, was anything listed in class 54 that the searcher may have overlooked? In figure 8.9, under the listing for *fly*, something called a net is classed in 54. Normally, one would visualize a fly net as something a butterfly collector would use to collect specimens, but remember the warning—terms in the index are true keywords and have no specific definitions. A fly net, because it is in class 54, must be some type of harness.

An experienced searcher would have located this right away. Professional searchers usually search only a handful of classifications in which they are expert and would know that class 54 would be the most obvious place to find a fly mask. An amateur searcher who was also the inventor of a fly mask would have found it too, because a *fly net* is another term for a fly mask.

This is not the end of the index search. Each term that was listed in step1 must be located in the index, if possible. Even though it seems as if an appropriate classification has been found the search is continued because patents do not carry just one class and subclass. Inventions are classed in several different areas that relate to individual components, and all possible classifications must be located before moving on to the next step. The *Manual of U.S. Patent Classification* in the next step and patent definitions in a later step will both give many classifications to search in locating a particular invention. When the searcher is finished with step 2, he or she should be armed with a handful of patent class and subclass numbers.

STEP 3
Consult the *Manual of U.S. Patent Classification*

The first two steps of the patent search were explained using the *Index to the U.S. Patent Classification*. Before beginning step 3, the patent searcher should have several possible classifications (class and subclass numbers) that relate to a particular invention. Even if a searcher is reasonably sure that a single correct classification has been found, all related classifications and subclassifications should be explored because a patent is placed not just in one classification, but in several. One of these is identified as the primary classification and the others as subclassifications. There is no strict rule as to which classification is the primary class. Patent examiners often just choose one as the primary class.

The *Manual of U.S. Patent Classification* is the beginning point of step 3. The manual is a two-volume set of three-ring, loose-leaf binders. All patent depository libraries and most government documents depository libraries have the index and the manual in their collections. The online version of the manual will be used here. It is located by going to www.uspto.gov, as was done in step 2 of this search process (see fig. 8.1), clicking on Patents to get to the services and resources page (see fig. 8.2), then clicking on Search Patents to get to the tools page (see fig. 8.3). This will produce the introductory page of the manual (see fig. 8.4). Or, as was recommended in the preceding step, if this page was bookmarked, simply go to that bookmark.

In the online manual, each classification is listed by number at the bottom of the introductory page (fig. 8.4). In the paper version of the manual, the subclassification numbers are listed in two columns on each page and include a two- or three-word description of that subclassification, but in the online version, just the class numbers are given.

In step 2, a fly mask was used to help explain the use of the index, and it was determined that a fly mask was most likely to be placed in class 54, titled Harness.

Figure 8.11 shows the beginning of class 54 as it is printed in the online manual. Definitions for the class may be seen by clicking on the class number, and subclass definitions may be seen by clicking on the subclass numbers in the column to the left as the searcher scrolls down the page. Figure 8.12 shows the page scrolled down to reveal some of the subclass terms and numbers. It is important to notice that the subclasses are not arranged in numerical order, but in rough numerical order as the class number relates to the technology. If a subclass is not listed in its logical place—for example, subclass 43 does not come between subclasses 42 and 44—look through the subclass listing for it. It will be there—unless it has been changed to another classification, which will be discussed in steps 4 and 5.

Recall from step 2 that the decimals used in classification numbers represent unique subclassifications. The plus sign (+), asterisk (*), and dot (.) also help refine a search. Refer to Figure 8.10 where the listing for *horse* is shown as it appears in the online index.

Horse/Boots/Design is listed as class D30, subclass 146+. Obviously this is a design patent in class 30, but the plus sign after the subclass number is puzzling. As this is explained, also look at the example of the manual in figure 8.12.

In figure 8.12, notice that some of the subclasses are printed in all uppercase letters and that some are preceded by dots. (In the actual online manual, different colors are also used.) The subclasses in uppercase are

FIGURE 8.11

Class 54

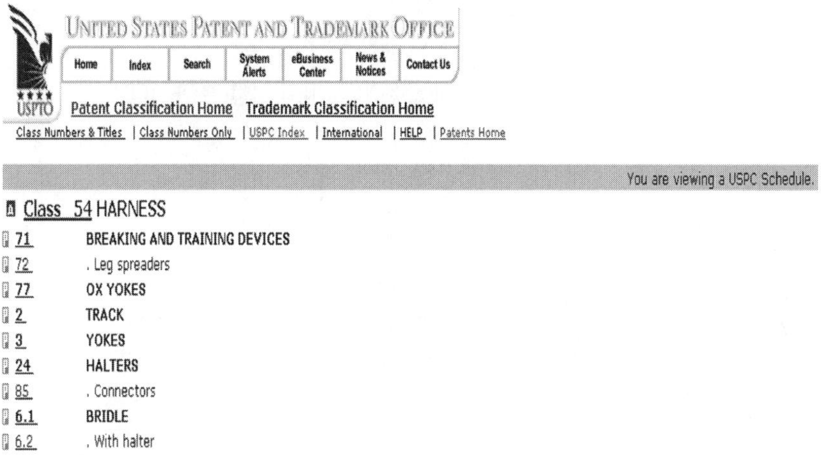

immediate subdivisions of the class—for example, subclass 24, Halters, is an immediate subdivision of class 54, Harness. Listings that are preceded by dots are further subdivisions of listings that are uppercase—for example, subclass 85, Connectors, is a subdivision of Halters, which is a subdivision of Harness. Listings with two dots preceding them are subdivisions of listings with one dot, and so on.

Class D30, subclass 146+ in figure 8.10 means that a searcher should look not only at D30/146, but at everything that has dots under 146 in the manual until the next uppercase listing is reached. For example, in figure 8.12, if the index had told the searcher to search 54/6.1+, the searcher would have to search 54/6.1, 54/6.2, 54/7, 54/8, and 54/9 because they are all preceded by dots. The search would continue until the next uppercase listing was reached. If the searcher skips step 3, those additional classifications would be missed.

The asterisk (*) after some subclass numbers is added more as a benefit for the patent examiner than for the patent searcher, but understanding it will aid the searcher in understanding the structure of the classification system.

The asterisk (*) is an indication of what the PTO calls a "cross-reference art collection." This has nothing to do with paintings or sculpture. To

FIGURE 8.12
Subclasses of Class 54

Subclass	Title
ClassTitle	===> HARNESS
71	▢ BREAKING AND TRAINING DEVICES
72	▢ . Leg spreaders
77	▢ OX YOKES
2	▢ TRACK
3	▢ YOKES
24	▢ HALTERS
85	▢ . Connectors
6.1	▢ BRIDLE
6.2	▢ . With halter
7	▢ . Bits
8	▢ .. Mouthpieces
9	▢ ... Double
10	▢ . Blinds
11	▢ .. Covering and uncovering
12	▢ . Brow bands
13	▢ . Crown loops
14	▢ . Gag runners
15	▢ . Stranglers
57	▢ UNDERCHECKS
16	▢ CHECKREINS
17	▢ . Hook loops
61	▢ CHECKHOOKS
62	▢ . Movable keeper
70	▢ CHECKING AND UNCHECKING DEVICES
35	▢ MARTINGALES
36	▢ REINS
74	▢ REIN HOLDS
63	▢ TERRETS

the PTO, an art collection is a collection of patents relating to a particular technology, or art. For example, buttons may be made by molding plastic, by carving wood, by stamping out metal disks, or by any of many methods. Because the subclasses are arranged by technology, each method of button making would be placed in a subclass that relates to the technology used to manufacture it. A patent examiner searching for button patents would have a difficult time locating all the appropriate subclasses; to make it easier, the examiner creates an art collection. Art collections are digests, or collections of patents from various classes, and are official subclasses. An art collection for the button-making example would contain only button-making patents from other classes placed in the digest by patent examiners to represent the variety of ways in which buttons can be manufactured. When an examiner is considering a button patent, the art collection acts as an index pointing to other classifications where button patents reside. A searcher can use the art collection in the same way to cross-reference an existing patent to several classification areas.

Figure 8.13 is an example of a page from the online index that has a lot going on in it. This index page shows an example of an alphabetic subclass number (Train Hotbox 246/169A), examples of subclasses with a plus sign (+) after them, design classes (D24/207, Hot Water Bottle Design), a cross-reference art collection (383/901 *), and a digest (053/DIG 1, Hot Dog Packaging). The DIG abbreviation in the hot dog packaging example stands for *digest*. A digest is the same as a cross-reference art collection except that it is *not* an official subclass. It is an informal index to other related patents.

The title of class 53, which a searcher would learn from consulting the

FIGURE 8.13

Sample Page from the Online Index

```
                          - - - - HOSPITAL FURNITURE AND EQUIPMENT
                          - - - - . (SEE TYPE)
        126 / 99R         - - - - HOT AIR FURNACE
        116 / 214         - - - - HOT BEARING INDICATOR
        246 / 169A        - - - - . . TRAIN HOTBOX
        047 / 19          - - - - HOT BED
        432 / 214    + - - - - HOT BLAST STOVES
                          - - - - HOT DOG
        D07 / 323    + - - - - . . COOKER
        053 / DIG 1       - - - - . . PACKAGING
        047 / 17     + - - - - HOT HOUSES
        180 / 68.3        . - - - - . . ENGINE COOLING VENTS
        D29 / 118    + - - - - HOT PAD OR MITT
        219 / 443.1  + . - - - - HOT PLATE
        D07 / 362    + - - - - . . DESIGN
        164 / 122    + - - - - HOT TOPPING
        249 / 106         - - - - HOT TOPS
        383 / 901    * - - - - HOT WATER BOTTLE
        D24 / 207    + - - - - . . DESIGN
        122               - - - - HOT WATER FURNACE
        324 / 106         - - - - HOT WIRE METERS
                          - - - - HOUNDS
```

manual, is Packaging. *Packaging* is also the keyword that the index uses to describe the type of patents that belong in class 53. The DIG means that patents in this group, 53/DIG 1, are patents that relate just to the packaging of *hot dogs*. They are assigned a DIG category because an examiner has placed a representative sample of hot dog packaging patents here to aid in a search where many different subclasses need to be searched. A DIG subclass may contain only one patent.

In figure 8.13, the Hot Water Bottle is an art collection and an official subclass. Hot Dog Packaging is a digest and not an official subclass. Both the art collection and digests may be found in the paper version of the manual at the end of the normal listings of patent classes. They can be found in the online manual by clicking on the number, which leads to a listing of digests by patent number.

The Rationale of the Manual

At this point, a searcher may ask why it is necessary to consult the manual at all, because the class/subclass numbers were already given in the index. Is anything learned in step 3 that wasn't learned in step 2? The answer is yes.

In step 2, the searcher progressed to the point at which there was a good indication that what the PTO called a *fly net* was the fly mask the searcher was seeking. But there was no verification of that. If the manual showed that a fly net was listed under insect-catching devices rather than with harness, the searcher would know that the term was a dead end. Without this verification from the manual, the searcher would waste time searching an unrelated group of patents.

Another reason to use the manual is that keywords are listed in the index without regard to definition, so it is often unclear what the listing means. In the fly mask example, figure 8.9 shows the listings from the index under the keyword *fly*. What is a *closer lasting tool?* Could it be some esoteric term for a fly mask? To find out, a searcher would consult class 12/113 in the manual and discover that a closer lasting tool is grouped with other patents relating to the manufacture of shoes. It is not related to the fly mask that is being sought, but by using only the index this information is not clear. The index and the manual should be used together in a patent search. In the Public Search Room of the PTO in Arlington, Virginia, the index and manual are bound together on special stands throughout the room because searchers use them in tandem. The online versions of both tools lead the searcher first to the manual by clicking Tools to Help in Searching by Patent Classification (fig. 8.3). A link from the manual introductory page then leads to the index, indicating that the manual is often used by experienced searchers without consulting the index at all.

Figure 8.14 shows the page in the online manual where the fly net is listed. It is categorized as class 54, subclass 80.4. Although the manual is designed to show technological relationships and to assist in the definition of the vague terms listed in the index, that is not always the case. Searchers finish using the manual in the same place they were when they finished the index—with a handful of class/subclass numbers. But there is a way to define exactly what a subclass includes.

STEP 4
Check Classification Definitions

In the preceding step, patent searchers used the *Manual of U.S. Patent Classifications* to verify that the class and subclass numbers, identified through the index, were accurate. However, for the fly mask invention, there was no clear indication that what the Patent and Trademark Office

FIGURE 8.14
Subclass Listing for Fly Net

78	TAIL HOLDERS
79.1	BLANKET OR GARMENT
79.2	. With retaining means
79.3	. With padding
79.4	. Specific material
80.1	BONNET OR SHIELD
80.2	. Eye shield
80.3	. Nose guard
80.4	. Fly net
80.5	. . Face guard
82	HORSE BOOTS
83.1	SPUR
83.2	. Adjustable to operative position
84	SUPPORTS
1	MISCELLANEOUS

listed as a "fly net" was actually the fly mask being searched. The only indications that the searcher was on the right track were (1) the fly net was grouped with other inventions in a class called Harness and (2) the fly net was a further subclass under the subclass Bonnet or Shield (fig. 8.14).

Step 4 guides the searcher through classification definitions, which are a dictionary of the class and subclass groups used by the PTO. This step is not always necessary. As was pointed out in step 3, usually the manual gives sufficient information to verify that the classifications about to be searched are accurate, but the fly mask classification is still vague after completing step 3, so this next step must be taken.

At the PTO, patent definitions are kept on printed sheets. Patent examiners are able to make changes and corrections to the classification directly on the paper sheets—more about that later. In patent and trademark depository libraries, the definitions are kept on microfiche cards that are updated periodically, so immediate changes in definitions are not known. On the PTO website www.uspto.gov, patent class definitions are given at the beginning of each main class page, as can be seen in figure 8.15. This shows class 54, labeled as Harness. If the searcher scrolls down the subclass list (fig. 8.14) and clicks on subclass 80.4, the result is the page shown in figure 8.16.

At this point, it may be helpful to note the difference between using patent definitions in a digital format and using them in a micro format. The preferred method is to use the online version because updates and changes are recorded more quickly than they are on the microfiche. But if a searcher finds herself confronted with microfiche in a patent depository library, an explanation of how to use the microfiche may be helpful.

Each microfiche card of the definitions contains one class, so, given that there are about four hundred classes, there are about four hundred pieces of fiche. Each fiche lists the definition for that class and the definition for each subclass within that class, in the same manner as is shown in figures 8.15 and 8.16.

Definition means that the class or subclass is defined in much the same way that a dictionary would define a term, except here the function is explained and examples are given. *Function* is basic to all patent searches and can be best explained by the following example.

Ovens can be of several types: gas, electric, or microwave. Logically, patents related to ovens of any type would be grouped in a class called Food and Beverage Apparatus, class 99. But because of the concept of *function*, each type of oven is classified with those patents that operate in a similar way. Gas ovens will be classed with other inventions that operate

FIGURE 8.15
Class Page from Online Manual

Class 054

HARNESS

Class Definition:
This class includes, besides the usual harness for attaching animals to vehicles, such harness arrangements or devices in connection with harnessed animals as are used for breaking or training animals, preventing their kicking; also horse-boots, riding saddles, spurs, ox-yokes, fly-nets, and such bonnets and protectors or shields for protecting the animal from sun, rain, etc., as are adapted to be attached to the animal or the harness; also, blanket- fasteners when not useful in other relations; also all pad, collar, and hame fasteners, halter, hame, and trace, trace and whiffletree couplings, and trace- carriers, generally relating to working animals.
General Note: Wherever the drawings are associated with the definitions, they are merely used to illustrate the basic concept encompassed by the definition of that subclass and should not be construed as limiting the scope of the subject matter covered by that subclass.

LINES WITH OTHER CLASSES AND WITHIN THIS CLASS
Patents relating solely to harness buckles, hooks, clips, clamps, clasps, couplings or fastenings of a general nature are in Class 24, Buckles, Buttons, Clasps, etc.
Holdback-hooks and other fastening devices especially adapted to secure the hold-back straps to the thills are in Class 278, Land Vehicles: Animal Draft Appliances, subclasses 127+.

REFERENCES TO OTHER CLASSES

SEE OR SEARCH CLASS:
40, Card, Picture, or Sign Exhibiting, subclass 303 for indicia in the form of letters, symbols, etc., carried by harness parts.
119, Animal Husbandry, subclasses 712+ for a device for controlling, restricting, or handling an animal, subclasses 850+ for body worn protective apparel, and subclasses 856+ for a body- or appendage-encircling device.
280, Land Vehicles, subclass 290 for body harness for the occupant of a velocipede.

---

on gas (primarily classes 126, 239, and 431). Electric ovens will be classed with electric devices that function by creating resistance in a metal coil causing electron friction which generates heat (class 219/391+); and microwave ovens will be classed with radar devices that scan with microwaves (class 219/678). Of course, some ovens will be grouped in a cross-reference art collection (see step 3). This explanation is given here not to muddy the waters, but to reemphasize that logically placing similar devices into a single category without regard to function will lead to frustration in a patent search.

For example, under class 446, toys, is the subclass 34 (see fig. 8.17). In the manual, subclass 34 is simply explained as AEROdynamically Supported or Retarded, meaning all types of aerial toys are classed here. The definition

FIGURE 8.16

Subclass Definitions

☐ 80.4   **Fly net:**

This subclass is indented under <u>subclass 80.1</u>. Subject matter consisting of a fabric made of threads, cords, or ropes woven or knitted together at regular intervals such as a mesh or screen used for protecting an animal against insects.

A-Body of fly net; B-Fly net strings; C-Straps

SEE OR SEARCH THIS CLASS, SUBCLASS:

<u>75,</u>   for covered trimmings, and 79.1 for a blanket or a garment.

---

gives this explanation: "Device including a surface which, when moved relative to the surrounding air, reacts with the air to either support the weight of the device, or to restrict its velocity."

But that is not all it says. Beneath the definition is the message "See or Search This Class, Subclass." Subclass 88 for model airplanes is then listed, meaning that if the searcher is looking for a model that really doesn't fly (although this class is for toys that *do* fly), he or she should check subclass 88 of class 446 because although model airplanes are aerial toys, their operation is different. Or, if the invention is a toy that looks like it should fly but really does not, subclass 237+ should be checked. (The plus sign used here was explained in step 2.) The searcher is also advised to consult an entirely different class, class 40/413, for hood ornaments that look like aircraft (yes, there is an entire subclass just for automobile hood ornaments that look like aircraft).

Although helpful most of the time in giving clear examples of the types of inventions that fit in various classes and subclasses, the definitions can also be confusing. This can be seen in the last sentence of the subclass 34 definitions:

FIGURE 8.17
Definitions for a Subclass

---

34 AERODYNAMICALLY SUPPORTED OR RETARDED:
    This subclass is indented under <u>the class definition</u>. Device including a surface which, when moved relative to the surrounding air, reacts with the air to either support the weight of the device, or to restrict its velocity.

SEE OR SEARCH THIS CLASS, SUBCLASS:

88,   for a model airplane adapted to be assembled from a kit, and with no aerodynamic features.

237+,   for a simulated aerial device (i.e., nonflying).

SEE OR SEARCH CLASS:

40,   Card, Picture, or Sign Exhibiting, subclass 413 for an automobile hood ornament in the form of an aircraft and which is caused to rise by the relative wind.

124,   Mechanical Guns and Projectors, for a centrifugally or mechanically operated device, per se, for launching a projectile into the air (e.g., a sling, bow, baseball or tennis ball pitching machine, slingshot, etc.).

244,   Aeronautics, appropriate subclasses for kites, and full size aeronautic devices. Inventions which apply logically to full size devices for actual use in carrying persons or cargo are classified in Class 244. All other toy or model aircraft are classified in Class 446.

Also included in Class 473 are (a) a centrifugally or mechanically operated device for projecting or launching such aerial projectile provided only that it is claimed in combination with at least one other game component such as a game projectile, (b) a player held and powered implement, per se, for striking and thereby projecting such aerial projectile, and (c) an implement or device, per se, for both projecting and catching an aerial projectile.

Anyone reading this definition would be more confused than helped.

The definitions, then are a mixed blessing. While they pin down exactly what fits into a subclass, they also give the searcher other places in the classification to search. This means that if a searcher had only one classification for her invention before checking the definitions, she will probably have several others to check when finished.

In the definition for the fly mask, class 54/80.4, the searcher will run into good luck (see fig. 8.16). The definition is direct: "fabric made of threads, cords, or ropes woven or knitted together at regular intervals such as a mesh or screen used for protecting an animal against insects." There are minimal "See or Search This Class, Subclass" notes or "See or Search Class" suggestions, and the ones that are there are very clear. This gives the searcher the information needed to continue. Inventions within 54/80.4 are nets used to protect animals from insects, and this is exactly the function of the invention being sought. Eureka!

Fortunately, when searchers have completed these first four steps, they have left behind the most difficult part of the search. Steps 1–4, comprising what is called the field of search or the location of the proper classification, can be confusing and frustrating to an amateur searcher. The next step, step 5, is the beginning of the prior art search. Prior art is less confusing, but more time-consuming. It is also fortunate that the PTO's online site allows a searcher to generate lists of patents within a particular class/subclass group instantly. As was shown in the field of search, however, there are symbols to understand and procedures to follow.

THE PATENT CLASSIFICATION SYSTEM
AS A LIVING ORGANISM

A bit of background is helpful at this point. Searchers should not think of the patent classification system as a static list like the Library of Congress Classification System. The patent classification system is a growing, changing thing. As technologies change or are absorbed by other technologies, the classification changes to reflect that.

In biological classification, a newly discovered animal is classed with other known animals having similar characteristics and, as much as it can, the patent classification system does that. But because completely new inventions occur, new classifications must be added, and an invention that previously fit into an existing class might have to be moved to a new class that more closely defines its function.

The PTO notifies searchers of these changes in two ways. First, the PTO regularly sends a listing of all changes, including any added or deleted classes, to all patent and trademark depository libraries. Second, the online classification tools—the index, the manual, and the definitions—are changed. This is not a rare occurrence; it happens hundreds of times a year. The classification system, like a living organism, is growing and changing daily.

A searcher who uses the PTO instead of a depository library should be aware that not all patents are kept in the Public Search Room. Certain entire classifications that show little activity over a given time are removed from the stacks and placed in storage in another building. Patent classes do age and die in their own way. New subclassifications are continually added, so there are births too.

It is sometimes difficult to envision how such an extensive patent classification system with over 400 classes and 104,000 subclasses does not already have a class designated for every new invention. But consider the photocopy machine. A dry copying process was the idea of a single inventor, Chester Carlson, and was a completely new technology when he got the inspiration in the 1930s. It differed from other copying processes in that previous copying processes used wet solutions to copy from a master. "Electrophotography," as the new process was called, did not use wet solutions.

Electrophotography did not use chemical solutions, but reproduced images using an electrical charge to attract the ink to the paper and then heated a plastic "ink" to attach the image to a piece of paper. This was not photography, not wet reproduction, and not anything that fit into existing electronic classifications. A change in the classification system had to be made for this completely new process and, in 1937, the first electrophotography patent was granted to Carlson.

Chapter 9

Patent Searching:
Determining the Prior Act

Previous steps have guided the patent searcher through what is called the field of search. The field of search identifies the proper classifications in which to locate a particular patent. The field of search, even for an experienced searcher, is confusing and carries with it the potential for mistakes and misinformation. Step 5 begins the prior art search. Prior art identifies patents in the designated classifications and leads to actual viewing of patent documents. Prior art is easier in some ways than field of search but is more time-consuming.

STEP 5
Review the Subclass List

There are two ways to begin step 5. One way is to use the subclass list online; the other is to use the CD-ROM product called CASSIS distributed by the PTO and available at all patent depository libraries (see appendix 1 for a list of these libraries). CASSIS is an acronym for the Classification and Search Support Information System and consists of a series of searching tools. CASSIS for searching subclass lists is a compact disc index that runs on a personal computer and is the quickest way to obtain a hard copy of an up-to-date subclass list. The searcher simply types in the patent class/subclass.

Officially, the subclass list is called the Classification Sequence—Subclass Listing or the U.S. Patent Classification—Subclass Listing and may be found in library catalogs under one of these headings. For the sake of brevity, here it will be called the subclass list. At government documents depositories and at the PTO in Washington, D.C., the subclass list is on a CD-ROM. On the Web, the subclass list is at www.uspto.gov. On the CD or the Web, the class and subclass sets are given in numerical order, and under each appears the patent numbers that are classed in that set. Design patents, if there are any in a given subclass, are listed after the utility patent numbers. For example, the subclass list on the CD for 54/80.4—the class/subclass for the fly mask search performed in the previous steps would look like figure 9.1.

To get to the subclass list from www.uspto.gov, follow the steps for locating the proper class for an invention. At the point where the patent subclass definitions are listed (fig. 8.16), click on the subclass number—54/80.4. The result is a list of patent numbers and titles in descending numerical order. An abbreviated method is to click a class from the class listings (fig. 8.4) and click a subclass number from the resulting page (fig. 8.12). Then click the subclass number from the resulting definitions page (fig. 8.16).

Following the patent number is an O or an X. The X means that this patent is a secondary classification. In previous steps the searcher was told that patents are placed not in just one classification, but in several. One classification is the primary class and the others are secondary or cross-reference classifications. A patent number with an X means that this is a secondary classification. If the searcher is searching more than one class/subclass, this patent number will appear again.

FIGURE 9.1

Subclass List

Classification: <u>54/80.4</u>   Ors: 18   XRs: 6   Total: 24

6128891 X 5440864 O 3803801 O 3778966 O 3104508 X 1840957 O 1728443 X

1715241 O 1543960 O 1516202 X 1488768 O 1318477 X 1183700 O 1159076 O

1113815 O 1110017 O 0836021 O 0826714 O 0645343 O 0584506 O 0481152 X

0378373 O 0284445 O 0073851 O

A U is an "unofficial" secondary subclassification and is not seen in the Web or CD versions of the subclass list. It still exists, however, in some of the older PTO products, such as microfilm subclass lists. The usage of any secondary classification is similar to the DIG category mentioned earlier. Examiners used to place a patent in this subclassification to act as an index to the many ways some things can be classified, but this practice has been discontinued. Because some of these U patent numbers still exist, however, a searcher may find patents marked with a U within a subclass that, when viewed, seem to be only marginally related to the other patents in the subclass. For example, the class/subclass list containing the fly mask, 54/80.4, also contains a patent for a potato digging machine. The potato machine patent is there because something about it relates directly to the class Harness, perhaps the fact that it is attached to a horse by means of a harness. The patent examiner wanted to be sure to cover this aspect when harness patents were searched.

The U, as mentioned earlier, no longer applies to current patents. Previously, examiners were allowed five official cross-references to be added to the original classification. If an examiner felt that additional cross-references were needed, such cross-references were given the U designation. In current practice, any classification in addition to the original classification carries an X designation. Supposedly these U classifications are being phased out, but they still will appear on subclass lists because the PTO is not removing them retrospectively. A searcher should treat X and U as equals of the primary classification and search all numbers listed on the subclass list.

Keeping Records

It is important that the searcher keep accurate records of the patent numbers that have already been viewed so that when the X number found in the cross-reference appears again in the listing of primary class patents, it is not necessary to view it again.

There is another reason to keep accurate records of what has been searched. Many searchers will complete the field of search, the subclass list, and a partial viewing of patents on their own, but hire an attorney to interpret certain complicated patents or to complete the search of patents in a subclass list. The attorney will want a record of what has been done up to that point. If the record is not complete and accurate, the attorney will duplicate the search already done, charging a per-hour rate, which defeats the purpose of performing a search by oneself.

Patent Attorneys, Agents, and Examiners

Lawyers are required to pass an examination given by the PTO to certify that they may practice patent law. A list of these patent attorneys can be found in most government document depository libraries and at all patent and trademark depository libraries in a volume titled *Attorneys and Agents Registered to Practice before the United States Patent and Trademark Office*. A somewhat easier way to locate a patent attorney is to look in the Yellow Pages under "Patent Attorneys."

Attorney's services and fees vary greatly according to geography, the type of patent being searched (some take longer than others), whether the attorney is handling the entire procedure or just a part of it, and the amount of haggling the attorney and the patent examiner get into when the application is examined. In all cases, however, the attorney will have to be a registered patent attorney.

The example of patent attorney fees shown in figure 9.2 is representational and may vary depending on the variables mentioned earlier. The office action fee and the filing fee are concurrent. That is, the filing fee is paid about twenty-four months after the patent application is filed, not twenty-four months after the office action. Even if a search is done completely without an attorney, an inventor will still have to pay $2,330.00 (allowing for four drawings at $80 each) if a patent attorney is used to prepare and file the patent application.

FIGURE 9.2

Representative Patent Attorney Fees

Service	Time	Cost
Patentability search and Prior Art search	4–5 weeks	$200–$300
Patent application	3–4 weeks	$1,100
Prepare drawings		$80/drawing
Filing fee		$170
Office action prosecution	10–12 months	$400+
Final issue fee	18–24 months	$340

Patent agents may also perform patent searches and file patent applications. A patent agent must pass the same written test as a patent attorney and also must have a specified amount of professional training in engineering. The difference is that a patent agent is not a lawyer. An agent is somebody trained in patent law and procedures, but has not passed the bar exam.

Patent examiners, those employees of the PTO who determine whether an invention is new, need not be attorneys either. Patent examiners are among the best-educated people in the federal bureaucracy, with many holding doctorates in technical fields. A problem in recent years is that patent examiners frequently attend law school in the evenings at government expense, then leave the government and practice patent law after they have graduated.

CASSIS

Although CASSIS is fairly simple to use, searchers who have never used it before will need an introduction. Librarians at patent and trademark depository libraries (PTDLs), the only libraries with CASSIS access, are trained in its use; therefore, what CASSIS does and how it does it will not be detailed here. Librarians not trained in CASSIS should consult a nearby PTDL (see appendix 1 for a listing) for instruction.

CASSIS does many things for patent searchers and does them quite well. If a searcher has a patent number, CASSIS can generate a list of all its classifications. This is helpful if a searcher knows of an existing patent that is similar to the one being searched. By inputting that patent number, the searcher can obtain a list of possible class/subclass groupings. This is a real time saver from the usual field of search procedure.

CASSIS can display a page from the manual, display only those subclasses having the same level of indentation (refer to step 3 and the dots preceding a subclass), search keywords within classification titles and in patent abstracts, search terms that appear in the index (see step 2), and, in more recent patents, display patent titles and names of companies having rights to the patent.

What to Do with a Subclass List

When a searcher obtains a subclass list of patent numbers, the next step is to obtain those patents on the list. There are hundreds of patents to look at, given that a searcher has one to ten subclass lists and each list contains at least one hundred patents. There are three methods of wading through this list, and each is described briefly here.

THE OG METHOD

The *Official Gazette of the United States Patent and Trademark Office* (OG) is published each Tuesday. In it the patents granted during the previous week are listed in numerical order and grouped by class/subclass. Although the entire patent is not reproduced in the OG, the gazette will contain a brief abstract and usually a reduced patent drawing. This is a popular search technique because over 450 libraries receive the OG and the patents may be scanned quickly. The spine of the OG lists the patent numbers included in that issue.

THE CASSIS METHOD

Patents are listed by number on a series of CD-ROMs in a section of CAS-SIS called USPAT. Both text and drawings are available. CASSIS is available at all PTDLs and in the Public Search Room at the PTO. The trick is to get the correct CD that contains the patent numbers a searcher is seeking. Patents can also be downloaded from CASSIS, so bring a disk. Ask the librarian to demonstrate the system and to point out the correct CDs for your search.

THE PTO METHOD

This is the preferred method, although its obvious disadvantage is that one must travel to the Patent and Trademark Office (PTO) in Washington, D.C. Patents are in paper booklets that are printed at the time the patent is issued and are grouped at the PTO into class/subclass arrangement. Most patent attorneys and agents use the PTO method.

STEP 6
Locate Patents by Number

In step 5, searchers were shown how to obtain a patent subclass listing. The subclass listing identifies patent numbers appearing in a given class/subclass group. Because only the number of the patent is given, the next step shows how to locate the actual patent by using the patent number.

Step 6 is actually a set of steps. There are three ways to locate patents by number and each method can be used by itself or combined with other methods. The primary consideration in choosing a search method is the type of patent depository the searcher is using. There are three types of patent depositories. The most common is a government documents depository library, which is usually part of a large public or academic library. The others are patent and trademark depository libraries (PTDLs) and the Patent and Trademark Office (PTO) itself. A CASSIS search, described below in this chapter, can be completed only at the PTO or at a PTDL.

Government Documents Depositories

Government documents depositories are located in over 450 libraries in the United States. Each depository collects documents published by the federal government and makes them available to the public. Each library collects a percentage of those things that the government identifies as depository items. Some standard depository items are the patent tools that have been described previously—that is, the index, the manual, and the *Official Gazette*. These libraries will not carry actual patents, but by using the *Official Gazette* (OG) a searcher may initiate a patent search. The OG method explained later shows how to use the OG to locate patents by number.

Patent and Trademark Depository Libraries (PTDLs)

PTDLs are scattered across the United States. They differ from government documents depository libraries in that the PTDLs carry a backfile of at least twenty years of patents. The patents are available on CASSIS rather than in paper copy. The PTDL search method described later is the most convenient for patent searchers, but can be very time-consuming.

The Patent and Trademark Office (PTO)

The PTO is the only practical place to perform a comprehensive patent search. However, the PTO is not convenient for the majority of patent searchers because it is in Washington, D.C. (Actually, the PTO is located in Crystal City, an office and commercial center across the Potomac in Arlington, Virginia.) Most searchers find that a search initiated at another location and completed at the PTO is most effective. The pros and cons of a PTO search are discussed in the following section.

Advantages and Disadvantages of the Three Search Methods

THE CASSIS METHOD

CASSIS was described in step 5 as an automated system that provides patents in a given class/subclass group. In addition to giving patent numbers, in listings of patents in a subclass, CASSIS gives the title of the patent first. This feature can be used by a searcher to quickly eliminate patents that, by their title, have no relation to the invention being searched. All unrelated patents cannot be eliminated this way, but this method is effective in reducing the number of actual patents that need to be viewed in their full format at a PTDL or at the PTO.

Of course, this is chancy because patent titles sometimes give no indication of what the patent is about. The CASSIS title method is not a technique for a comprehensive search, but it is a tool for reducing hundreds of patents in the group of class/subclass areas that a searcher is examining. As may be seen in the PTDL and PTO methods, any reduction in the number of patents to be viewed can save many hours of search time. As noted earlier, CASSIS is available only at PTDLs and at the PTO.

THE OG METHOD

The Official Gazette method uses the *Official Gazette of the United States Patent and Trademark Office* (OG). The advantage of this method is that it can be used at any of the government documents depositories described earlier. The OG is published every Tuesday and contains all the patents issued during the previous week. However, it does not contain the actual patent but rather an abstract of what is patented and usually a single drawing of the invention.

Armed with a list of patent numbers, a searcher would go through each weekly issue of the OG and eliminate unrelated patents in much the same way as the CASSIS method. The advantage here is that the searcher is working not only with a title, but also with a description and a picture. The OG method is not a comprehensive search method, but, like the CASSIS method, its purpose is to reduce the number of actual patents that need to be viewed in their full format.

The obvious disadvantage is that there are fifty-two OGs each year. Even a minor search of patents in a given class/subclass group for the previous ten years would mean that a searcher would be handling 520 OGs—a very time-consuming and tedious task.

THE PTDL METHOD

Once a searcher has a list of patent numbers, the PTDL allows the searcher to go directly to the patents for viewing without the slow downloading associated with web-based tools. Patents at PTDLs are not in a paper format (with only two or three exceptions). The CDs are arranged by patent number, so the searcher need only locate the CD that contains the number being sought. The CD is a full duplication of the paper copy of the patent and contains all drawings. As mentioned earlier, this is the most convenient method for most amateur searchers because there is a PTDL in most states.

THE PTO METHOD

This is the only comprehensive, simple method of searching a large number of patents. At the PTO, paper copies of patents are arranged in class/subclass groups and placed in their own compartments, called "shoes." (Recall from chapter 6 that Thomas Jefferson, the first patent commissioner, kept copies of patents in his old shoe boxes.) A searcher has only to walk to open shelving containing the shoes, pull the appropriate classification, and easily flip through the paper copies to perform a search. The PTO even provides custom-made V-shaped stands that allow searchers to view the patents vertically.

Searchers should be aware that although it is commonly believed that all patents are housed in the Public Search Room of the PTO, they are not. The fly mask classification 54/80.4, for example, is considered an inactive classification and is housed outside the Public Search Room, but it is in paper and readily available.

The Importance of the Prior Art Search

Something should be said here about the importance of a prior art search and the amount of time that an amateur searcher should reasonably spend on it. A searcher makes a search to verify that an invention is not already patented. There is no penalty for submitting an application to the PTO for a device that is already patented; however, the money spent for making the application and preparing the drawings and the time spent in preparing the application will be lost if the PTO finds that a patent already exists for the invention being submitted. An inventor who has performed the search and prepared the application materials without any assistance from a patent attorney or agent would lose about $600.

Some inventors are willing to risk an application without performing a search at all, although the PTO requires that a listing of class/subclass groups searched be included on the patent application. This is not as bizarre as it sounds. Even though an amateur searcher or an attorney has performed what is considered a comprehensive search, the PTO performs its own search. If the PTO finds an existing patent, the applicant will lose all fees. An inventor must weigh the potential risk of losing the application fees against the time or money spent in searching prior patents.

Eliminating Unrelated Patents

After deciding on a search method, a searcher should know how to eliminate patents that are not related to the invention being searched. This part of the search requires some skill and familiarity with the technology that created the invention being searched. Being able to view a patent and make a decision quickly on its relationship to another invention is a valuable skill.

Recall the fly mask invention. The searcher should ask, What is it about this particular fly mask that makes it unique and patentable? Is it made with a unique design? Is it fastened to the animal in a unique way? Does it adjust to fit all sizes of animals? If there are several unique features in an invention, the searcher should focus on one item at a time until getting the hang of searching. The fly mask being searched has one unique feature—the straps that hold it in place are designed such that the mask can fit any type of animal, whether it be a sheep, a cow or a horse. This then is the focus of the search.

Amateur searchers have one advantage over professional patent searchers. The amateur searcher is likely also the inventor of the device. The unique features of an invention are well known to the inventor and, because the inventor is working with one particular technology, it also is very familiar. For example, the inventor of the fly mask knows how a strap must be fixed to the mask and what features of a strap make it adjustable. When such a searcher is going through class 54/80.4, the fly mask classification, it is readily apparent whether an existing patent has the unique features of the new invention.

Patent attorneys usually do not search the patents at the PTO themselves. They hire professional searchers in the Washington, D.C., area to perform searches for them. These professionals search a wide spectrum of classifications. Although these professional searchers are very good at what they do, they didn't invent the fly mask and must depend on documentation from or communication with the patent attorney to determine what is unique about the patent being searched. The amateur is usually quicker and more aware of subtleties in existing patents.

Assume that the amateur has followed steps 1–6 and has identified a class, has a list of patent numbers, has eliminated a number of patents that seemed unrelated by using the OG, and is now seated in the PTO Public Search Room in Crystal City. Just what is it in the patent that a searcher is looking for? There are two primary items: the drawings and the claims.

STEP 7
Examine Patent Claims

Claims are the effective part of a patent. They are numbered paragraphs that give a precise description of the invention and list all its essential features. The claims are the basis for patent infringement suits because what is unique about an invention must be mentioned in the claims.

In disclosing a patent (that is, publishing the patent complete with drawings, descriptions, claims, and so on, as is done when a patent is granted), occasionally some unique feature is not claimed although it appears in the drawings. David Pressman, a noted patent writer, states that one may copy that part of the invention without liability because it is not described in the claims. It is important, therefore, that every unique feature of an invention be accurately described in the claims.

Claims define the structure of an invention in precise terms. The legal protection given the patent is delineated by the claims and not by the drawings, disclosure, specifications, or any other part of the patent. Patent attorneys and agents are trained in the art of writing a claim narrow enough to show uniqueness, but broad enough to give an inventor some protection from other, similar inventions. The importance of the claims cannot be overstated.

What does this mean to a patent searcher and how can it help in the search process? In the fly mask example, the answer to the question What is unique about this particular fly mask? can be found in the claims. In the preceding step it was determined that one of the unique features of the fly mask invention being searched was the straps that enabled it to fit any type of animal. In viewing the actual patent, a searcher could look at the drawings to see if an existing fly mask patent had straps and, if it did, read the claim to see if the straps were adjustable and, if adjustable, determine if they adjust in the same manner as the fly mask being searched. The variations can be extensive. For example, are the adjustable straps connected with Velcro or with a buckle and does that make a difference in infringement? Inventors must make that determination for themselves and should not depend on a librarian to make it for them.

Librarians must take great care in explaining patent claims. Interpretation of claims gets into the fuzzy area of patent law, and a decision as to whether a particular claim is an infringement on an existing patent is a matter best left to patent attorneys and agents. Not only is this wise, but interpreting claims in other than a very broad explanatory sense constitutes the practice of law. Librarians and others assisting with a patent search must be careful to explain what the claims are, not interpret them. Medical librarians are familiar with this concept because they cannot diagnose an illness for a library user or recommend treatment.

Following is one of the claims in patent 3,803,801. This patent for a fly mask, granted in 1974, is one of only five patents in class 54/80.4 granted in the past nineteen years.

What I claim and desire to secure by Letters Patent is:

1. An insect control device for animals and comprising:

   a. a band adapted to be placed around a neck portion of an animal;

   b. a nose strap secured to said band and adapted to extend at least partially around a nose portion of the head of the animal;

   c. a head strap connected to said band and adapted to extend at least partially around the head of the animal and adjacent to the eyes thereof;

   d. a plurality of laterally spaced narrow substantially rigid strips mounted at one end thereof on said head straps and positioned to extend at least partially over the eyes of the animal;

   e. said band and nose strap and head strap are each adjustable to conform to the respective portions of the head of the animal.

In 1.e. the patentee states that this fly mask is adjustable. When the searcher sees this, he or she should immediately look at the drawings that accompany the patent. Patent 3,803,801 has five drawings. One of them clearly shows an adjustable strap that connects by means of a buckle like those on belts. Is this adjustable strap close enough to the patent being searched that it constitutes an infringement? No decision can be made by a librarian. The searcher is also wise not to make a definite judgment at this point, but to place the patent in a group of questionable patents that will be generated during the search. This group of questionable patents should then be taken to a patent attorney or agent for an interpretation.

Patent 4,791,777 is the last patent granted in class 54/80.4. It was awarded on December 20, 1988, and has only a single claim:

1. A leg net assembly positionable about the leg portion of an animal to prevent insects from contacting the leg, said leg net assembly comprising: a central, generally cylindrical, loose fitting body portion . . . and upper and lower supports, said upper and lower supports each being formed of a knit, high stretch material and being attached to upper and lower ends, respectively of said central generally cylindrical body.

It is obvious that this fly net is designed to cover the legs and not the face of an animal. It is also obvious that the attachment to the animal is by stretch-fabric bands and not buckles or straps. A searcher will probably disregard this patent immediately as being unrelated to the fly mask being searched. For the librarian who may be helping a patent searcher, however, the important thing to remember is that no interpretation can be made. That is, if asked by the searcher if this patent is related or unrelated to the fly mask being searched, the librarian can give no answer. It is up to the searcher or the searcher's attorney to make that decision.

At this point in the search process, the librarian should let searchers proceed on their own. Interpretations, writing the patent, filing forms, and making drawings are best left to the inventors and their legal representatives.

An amateur patent searcher will leave the library having completed the search process and will have a small group of patents that can be shown to an attorney for interpretation.

SUMMARY OF THE PROCESS

The major steps to searching a patent are as follows:

STEP 1: Identify the parts of the invention.

Break the invention down. For example, a generator-driven electric light for a bicycle would include a light, a generator, and a bicycle. Think of as many synonyms or related terms as possible to identify the parts of the invention.

STEP 2: Consult the *Index to the U.S. Patent Classification.*

The keyword index will give a class and subclass for each term identified in step 1. When finished with this step, a searcher will have many sets of class/subclass numbers.

STEP 3: Consult the *Manual of U.S. Patent Classification.*

The manual will show the relation of the invention to other inventions within the same technology. It also provides the searcher with finer indexing of specific aspects of the invention, leading to more direct class/subclass listings.

STEP 4: Consult the *Patent Definitions*.

The wording in the index and manual is sometimes vague. This leads to some confusion as to whether the classifications the searcher has identified are correct. The definitions specifically state what type of device fits into every class and subclass. This is sometimes as confusing as the index and manual themselves, so it's good to know that many times this step can be skipped if searchers are fairly certain that they have the right classes.

STEP 5: Get a list of patents in each class/subclass group.

Once the classifications are identified, the list of patents in each class can be generated through CASSIS.

STEP 6: Eliminate each obviously unrelated patent.

There are four ways to do this: by going to the PTO in Washington and viewing actual patents, by scanning the *Official Gazette*, by scanning a CASSIS listing of titles to eliminate obviously unrelated inventions, or by using a patent depository library to view patents on CD-ROM.

STEP 7: Consult the claims to eliminate unrelated patents.

Claims state specifically what is new about the invention. By reading the claim, searchers can determine which patents can be kept and which disregarded as unrelated to the invention being searched. Those patents that are of questionable relationship to the patent being searched should be collected and a decision made about their relevance by the searchers themselves or by a patent attorney or agent.

One comfort in all this is the knowledge that the PTO will perform its own search to verify that a patent does not already exist. The searcher is going through this process because if the PTO does find a patent that the searcher has overlooked, the inventor will forfeit all application, preparation, and legal fees. As noted earlier, the search should not cost as much in fees and the searcher's time as the inventor stands to lose if an existing patent is found by the PTO.

Step 7 completes the librarian's role in offering assistance to an amateur patent searcher. By following the steps outlined in chapters 8 and 9 and by remembering the background knowledge presented, a librarian should be able to make a searcher feel confident and sure of the basic procedure in applying for a U.S. patent. Of course, there are many books, articles, and supplemental materials that will be useful to a searcher. When selecting an attorney, for example, the searcher will find the list of registered patent attorneys and agents helpful.

Many patent writers say that the U.S. patent system has effectively eliminated the individual inventor by making the process complicated and expensive. To a novice, a patent search can be an intimidating and confusing process. Clearly the system is not designed for amateurs and they are at a disadvantage, but it can be done. Thousands of amateur searchers each year perform their own searches. Unless the invention being searched is extraordinarily complicated, such as some recent electronic devices, even those with modest educational and legal backgrounds can succeed in completing the process.

The right to patent is guaranteed by the U.S. Constitution, which wisely gave that right to individuals and not to corporations. Unfortunately, unlike in previous times when a patent on a simple idea could make an individual wealthy, it is rare today to find individuals who are able to profit from patenting a simple device. However, both the federal government, through its Patent and Trademark Depository Library Program, which makes patents available to the public, and private enterprise, through such organizations as Invent America, which encourages school-aged children to invent patentable devices, are making an attempt to preserve the spirit of American ingenuity.

As noted earlier, the U.S. patent system is a living, changing thing. The process outlined here may change in the next few years as the PTO attempts to apply new technologies or changes the design of its Web pages. The patent system is also not free of controversy that may change search techniques or the manner in which patents are secured. Librarians should try to be aware of these changes as they occur.

Chapter 10

Trademarks

A good name, declares Scripture, "is more desirable than great riches" (Prov. 22:1). William Shakespeare wrote "Who steals my purse, steals trash. . . . But he that filches from me my good name, robs me of what not enriches him and makes me poor indeed" (*Othello*). A trademark is a name or a graphic representation of a name. As spelled out in Title 15 of the U.S. Code, it is either a word, phrase, symbol, or design, or a combination of words, phrases, symbols, or designs, that identifies and distinguishes the goods or services of one party from those of others. More simply stated, a trademark is a symbol or word that identifies something. For example, the Nike name and "swoosh" identify Nike products; the golden arches identify McDonald's restaurants.

A service mark is the same as a trademark except that it identifies and distinguishes the source of a service rather than a physical object. Throughout this chapter the terms *trademark* and *mark* are used to refer to both trademarks and service marks, whether they are word marks or other types of marks. Normally, a mark for goods appears on the product or on its packaging, while a service mark appears in advertising for the service.

A trademark is different from a copyright or a patent. A copyright protects an original artistic or literary work; a patent protects an invention. The differences are explained in detail in the first chapter of this book. The basis for current trademark law is the Lanham Act, passed in 1946. The Lanham Act is over fifty years old and unlike copyright law, has shown the power to adapt to changing technologies with only minor adjustments. The most significant changes in trademark law in the digital age affect the manner in which trademarks are searched and registered.

Unlike other forms of intellectual property, trademarks had to be used in commerce *before* protection was granted. But in 1988, the Trademark Law Revision Act (TLRA) eliminated that requirement. Before the TLRA, the Lanham Act required that a business or individual seeking to register a trademark in the United States make use of the mark in interstate commerce before applying for a registration. That is, in order to secure trademark protection, a businessperson could sell one of his or her products to a friend in the next state for a nominal fee. After showing proof that an interstate act of commerce had taken place, the businessperson would then be granted federal trademark protection. This interstate commerce provision of the law resulted in "token use," to comply with the letter, but not the spirit, of the law. To remedy this problem, a dual application system was created. It gave all applicants the choice of registering a mark on the basis of preapplication use in commerce, as they had done previously, or on the basis of a bona fide intention to use the mark in commerce in the future. Under the intent-to-use system, token use became obsolete.

The TLRA also contained a number of other provisions. To confront the problem posed by the volume of abandoned or inactive marks ("deadwood") on the trademark register, the duration and renewal periods for the registration of a mark were reduced from twenty to ten years.

BACKGROUND

The Lanham Act was not the first U.S. trademark law. Trademarks were used infrequently before the Civil War and received little attention from Congress or the states. During the Industrial Revolution, manufacturers sensed the need for product identity. This led to enactment of the first federal trademark law in 1870. The law was amended in 1878 and was soon declared unconstitutional by the Supreme Court on the grounds that the law was based improperly on the patent and copyright clause in Article 1, Section 8 of the Constitution.

In response, a group of manufacturers founded the International Trademark Association (INTA). The association's first order of business was to expedite enactment of the Trade-Mark Act of 1881 to resolve the unconstitutional issues of the 1878 law. In 1898, Francis Forbes, president of INTA, was named by President William McKinley to head a commission to revise the statutes relating to patents, trade and other marks, and trade and commercial names. The commission's report, submitted to Congress in 1900, reviewed the entire history of trademark protection and made recommendations that formed the basis of the Trade-Mark Act of 1905. The last major pre–Lanham Act revision to the federal trademark law was the Trade-Mark Act of 1920, the primary purpose of which was to implement international intellectual property commitments.

Congressman Fritz Lanham of Texas, on January 22, 1945, introduced the latest in a series of bills that he believed would encourage registration and protect marks from unfair competition. The bill defined a trademark as "any word, name, symbol, or device, or any combination thereof adopted by a manufacturer or merchant to identify his goods and distinguish them from those manufactured or sold by others." It further expanded the concept of infringement, permitted registration of service marks, provided contestability status for marks in continuous use for five years, and provided that federal registration of a trademark would constitute "constructive notice of the registrant's claim of ownership thereof." President Harry S. Truman signed the Lanham Act in 1946.

In 1967, trademarks received a well-deserved boost in status when Congress changed the name of the Patent Office to the Patent and Trademark Office. Congress believed that in light of the office's responsibility for administering both patents and trademarks, the former name was misleading.

One of the more interesting concepts in the new trademark law was the refusal to grant protection on marks that were considered immoral, scandalous, or deceptive. Because the interpretation of immorality is a slippery thing, some interesting challenges to trademarks have arisen. One of these concerns Procter and Gamble's moon and stars trademark. P&G's trademark originated in 1851, when many products did not carry a brand name. The original trademark was a star, which identified the company's candles, called Star Brand candles. The star became thirteen stars for the thirteen original colonies and a man-in-the-moon was added, looking out on the stars in the evening—the perfect time for candles. The trademark was officially registered with the U.S. Patent Office in 1882.

One hundred years later, in 1981, a rumor began that alleged that the trademark is a symbol of Satanism. Because Satanism, in the view of some, is immoral, several religious groups sought to have Procter and Gamble discontinue its trademark in accord with the immoral, scandalous, or deceptive element of the Lanham Act. The rumor involved a Procter and Gamble executive who discussed Satanism on a nationally televised talk show and indicated that P&G was somehow linked with the devil.

The rumor was shown to be totally false. Producers for the television programs mentioned in connection with the rumor confirmed that no one from P&G had ever appeared on their programs. Several nationally prominent religious leaders also called for an end to the false stories, calling them vicious and ludicrous. P&G filed over a dozen lawsuits to attempt to resolve the matter.

Other trademarks not protected by U.S. intellectual property laws include those that disparage institutions or beliefs or that incorporate flags or coats-of-arms. Trademarks with the name or image of a living person (without consent) or of a living president or of a dead president if his or her spouse is still living are also not protected.

LOSS OF TRADEMARK PROTECTION

Trademarks can be lost if the trademark falls into common usage. That is, if a new product is trademarked and becomes very successful, all subsequent versions of that product, even though produced by another manufacturer, tend to be called by the trademark of the pioneer product. If all brands of a given product are referred to by the trademarked name, the trademark becomes useless to the original manufacturer. In some lawsuits by trademark owners against those who have used a trademark illegally, the primary factor is proof that the general public and the media commonly use the trademark as a generic term.

The classic example of this is Kleenex. Although Kimberly-Clark, the owner of the trademark, still attempts to protect its trademark, the general public refers to all paper facial tissues as "kleenex." In the media, however, such as an advertising supplement in a daily newspaper, facial tissues cannot be referred to as kleenex unless they are Kleenex brand tissues. Corporations spend many millions of dollars annually protecting their trademarks in lawsuits against those who attempt to bring them into common usage.

A decade ago, Xerox Corporation mounted an extensive media campaign to inform the public that unless a document is copied on a Xerox machine, it is not a Xerox. It is a photocopy. Only a copy made on Xerox equipment can be referred to as a Xerox. The following registered trademarks used to identify only a particular brand of product but now are in common usage as generic terms for all items of the same type: Aspirin,

AstroTurf, Band-Aid, Baggies, Bundt, Cat Chow, Chablis, Cream of Wheat, Crock-Pot, Day-Timer, Dog Chow, Dumpster, Elevators (shoes), Foosball, Frisbee, Hula Hoop, Jacuzzi, Jet Ski, Kleenex, Laundromat, Lazer Tag, Little League, Nylon, Perrier, Photostat, Plexiglas, Poly-Fil, Popsicle, Post-it Notes, Radar, Realtor, Rollerblades, Rolodex, Seeing Eye Dog, Scuba, Shredded Wheat, Sno-Kone, StairMaster, Stetson, Styrofoam, Top-Siders, Valium, Varathane, Welcome Wagon, Wite-Out, X-Acto, Yo Yo, and, of course, Xerox.

In 1974, Ralph Anspach, a San Francisco State University economics professor, invented a game in which players made war on big business. He named it Anti-Monopoly after being told by his lawyer that this title was not an infringement of the Monopoly trademark because the "anti" added to "monopoly" would prevent confusion between the two games.

General Mills, which had bought Parker Brothers, the owner of the trademark Monopoly, insisted that it owned the brand name "monopoly." The company had already stopped Catholic laymen from marketing a game called Theopoly and others from marketing a game called Black Monopoly. A bitter legal war ensued between General Mills and Anspach that lasted for a decade. A federal district judge ruled for Monopoly twice and banned Anti-Monopoly from the market for six of those ten years. But Anti-Monopoly and Anspach fought back, won two appeals, and ultimately won in the U.S. Supreme Court. The Court held that the famous Monopoly trademark was generic and, hence, unprotectable. However, in 1984, Congress passed the Trademark Clarification Act which nullified the effect of the decision in *Anti-Monopoly, Inc. v. General Mills Fun Group, Inc.* and returned the Monopoly trademark to General Mills.

ESTABLISHING TRADEMARK RIGHTS

Trademark rights arise from either (1) actual use of the mark, or (2) the filing of a proper application to register a mark in the PTO stating that the applicant has a bona fide intention to use the mark in commerce regulated by the U.S. Congress. Federal registration is not required to establish rights in a mark, nor is it required to begin use of a mark. However, federal registration can secure benefits beyond the rights acquired by merely using a mark. For example, the owner of a federal registration is presumed to be the owner of the mark for the goods and services specified in the registration, and to be entitled to use the mark nationwide. The owner of a mark that is not registered is not automatically *presumed* to be its owner, only the party that is using the mark. A consumer can readily see the difference between a registered trademark and a trademark that is used but not registered. A registered trademark carries the symbol ®, whereas a nonregistered mark uses the symbol ™.

There are two related but distinct types of rights in a mark: the right to register and the right to use. Generally, the first party who either uses a mark in commerce or files an application in the PTO has the ultimate right to register that mark. The right to use a mark can be more complicated to determine. This is particularly true when two parties have begun use of the same or similar marks without knowledge of one another and neither has a federal registration. Only a court can render a decision about the right to use the mark.

Unlike copyrights or patents, trademark rights can last indefinitely if the owner continues to use the mark to identify its goods or services. The term of a federal trademark registration is ten years, with ten-year renewal terms. However, between the fifth and sixth years after the date of initial registration, the registrant must file an affidavit setting forth certain information to keep the registration alive. If no affidavit is filed, the registration is canceled.

TYPES OF APPLICATIONS FOR FEDERAL REGISTRATION

An applicant may apply for federal registration in three principal ways: (1) an applicant who has already commenced using a mark in commerce may file based on that use (a "use" application); (2) an applicant who has not yet used the mark may apply based on a bona fide intention to use the mark in commerce (an "intent-to-use" application); and (3) under certain international agreements, an applicant from outside the United States may file in the United States based on an application or registration in another country. For the purpose of obtaining federal registration, *commerce* means all commerce that may lawfully be regulated by the U.S. Congress—for example, interstate commerce or commerce between the United States and another country. The use in commerce must be a bona fide use in the ordinary course of trade, and not made merely to follow the letter of the law to reserve a right in a mark, as stated earlier.

A U.S. registration provides protection only in the United States and its territories. If the owner of a mark wishes to protect a mark in other countries, that owner must seek protection in each country separately under the relevant laws.

WHO MAY FILE AN APPLICATION?

The application must be filed in the name of the owner of the mark—usually an individual, a corporation, or a partnership. This differs from patents, which must be owned by one or more individuals. Corporations may not own a patent, but may have patent rights assigned to them. Additionally, trademarks cannot be owned anonymously as is possible with copyrights.

SEARCHES FOR CONFLICTING MARKS

An applicant is not required to conduct a search for conflicting marks before applying with the PTO. However, some people find it useful. In evaluating an application, an examining attorney conducts a search and notifies the applicant if a conflicting mark is found. The application fee, which covers processing and search costs, will not be refunded even if a conflict is found and the mark cannot be registered. In this way, trademarks are similar to patents.

To determine whether a conflict exists between two marks, the PTO first determines whether there would be likelihood of confusion—that is, whether relevant consumers would be likely to associate the goods or services of one party with those of the other party as a result of the use of the marks at issue. The principal factors to be considered in reaching this decision are the similarity of the marks and the commercial relationship between the goods and services identified by the marks. That means that similar marks may be used in different industries as long as there is no confusion in the mind of the consumer. However, to find a conflict, the marks need not be identical, and the goods and services do not have to be the same.

In 1986, Rose Art registered the trademark "Fun Dough" for its modeling clay. Kenner Parker Toys, which at the time owned the trademark "Play Doh" for its modeling clay, objected and filed suit in the U.S. Circuit Court of Appeals. Kenner won. Rose Art appealed to the U.S. Supreme Court, but the Court refused to hear the case.

Rose Art then attempted to register many variations on the name Play Doh, but with each attempt, Kenner filed suit. The matter seemed to be resolved in 1992 when the Circuit Court issued a strongly worded decision striking down Rose Art's Fun Dough trademark. That might have been the end of the issue except that in May 1992, the Patent and Trademark Office approved an application for the Fun Dough trademark that had been on file for a year. Hasbro, which bought Kenner Parker Toys and now owned the

Play Doh trademark, believed the approval of application was a mistake, but was unable to get the PTO to reverse its decision to register the trademark. Hasbro filed suit in U.S. District Court in Newark, New Jersey. Rose Art filed a countersuit, alleging that the name Play Doh had become generic and had fallen into common usage.

The resolution of this matter can be seen in any toy store by looking at the different brands of modeling clay on the shelves. Play Doh is proudly displayed with the ®, meaning that Play Doh is a registered trademark. Fun Dough is accompanied by the ™ symbol. This alternate ™ symbol means that Rose Art is using the product name as an unregistered trademark. The suit is still in court.

Another interesting trademark case also involves Hasbro. In 1995, a company called IEG acquired the Internet domain name Candyland.com. Most Americans as well as many people worldwide are aware of the famous board game for children called Candy Land. About 1.5 million of the games are sold worldwide annually. The trademark was registered for the game in 1951 and has been in continuous use since then. It is now owned by Hasbro. Trademark law, however, does in some cases permit the use of similar trademarks as long as the marks are used in different industries. The problem in this situation was that IEG wanted to use the mark Candyland for a sexually explicit Internet site.

Hasbro sued in 1995, stating that the use of the mark Candyland in connection with such a business tarnished the image of fun associated with Hasbro. Hasbro also pointed out that Candy Land was designed to appeal to small children. IEG pointed out that the mark Candy Land was already in use as a mark in other industries for a wide variety of goods and services, such as food, dolls, childcare services, and vending machines. Especially troubling was that Hasbro had intended to use the mark in a planned move into computer games. Hasbro managed to get a federal court to issue a preliminary injunction to stop IEG from using the name Candyland until the matter was resolved. In the final decision, which came in less than a year, Hasbro prevailed and stopped IEG from using the mark to advertise an adult website.

EXAMPLES OF INFRINGING MARKS

Here are two groups of pairs of trademarks. In one group, the two marks presented were determined to not be infringing marks. In the other set, the marks were determined to be infringing marks. The infringing set is identified at the end of the lists.

List 1

Ameribanc and Bank of America

Arise and Awake

Arm & Hammer and Arm in Arm

Arrow and Air-O

Aveda and Avita

Beauty-Rest and Beauty Sleep

Beck's Beer and Ex Bier

Beep and Veep

Blockbuster Video and Video Buster

Blue Nun and Blue Angel

Blue Shield and Red Shield

Blue Thunder and Blue Lightning

Brew Miser and Coffee Miser

Bust Rust and Rust Buster

Caesar's Palace and Trump's Palace

Cat Trac and Katrack

Century 21 and Century 31

Chat Noir and Black Cat

Citibank and City Bank

City Girl and City Woman

Coca-Cola and Cleo Cola

Comsat and Comcet

Cristóbal Colon and Christopher Columbus

Cyclone and Tornado

Datsun and Dotson

Dell and Bell

Dernier Touche and The Final Touch

Downtowner and Uptowner

Dramamine and Bonamine

El Gallo and The Rooster

Est Est Est and It Is It Is It Is

Face to Face and Cheek to Cheek

Firm 'n Gentle and Nice 'n Gentle

Gastown and Gas City

Gentle Touch and Kind Touch

Good Morning and Buenos Días

Heritage and Hermitage

Hint O'honey and Hidden Honey

Joujou and Jojo

Kahlúa and Chula

Knorr and Nor-King

Listerine and Listogen

London Fog and Smog

Lorraine and La Touraine

Manpower and Womenpower

Medi-Alert and Medic Alert

Mennen and Minon

Miracle Whip and Salad Whip

Mountain King and Alpine King

Nikon and Ikon

Old Forester and Old Foster

Orkin and Orko

Philadelphia and Pennsylvania

Pizzeria Uno and Taco Uno

Play Doh and Fun Dough

Pledge and Promise

Porsche and Porsha

Rain Barrel and Rain Fresh

Rockland Mortgage Corp. and Rockwell National Mortgage

Savings Shop and The Savings Spot

Seiko and Seycos

Silver Flash and Super Flash

Smirnoff and Sarnoff

Snappy and Snippy

S.O. and Esso

Sparkletts and Sprinklets

Squirt and Quirst

Steinway and Steinweg

Telechron and Telicon

Toro Rojo and Red Bull

Toys "R" Us and Kids "R" Us

Trak and Traq

Ultra Brite and Ultra-dent

Ultra Velvet and Ultra Suede

Weed Eater and Leaf Eater

Yamaha and Makaha

List 2

Accutron and Unitron

After Tan and Aprés Sun

Bank in a Billfold and Bank in a Wallet

Boston Tea Party and Boston Sea Party

Car-X and Exxon

Coca-Cola and Coco Loco

Coca-Cola and The Uncola

Cream of Wheat and Creamy Wheat

Dawn and Daylight

Duvet and Duet

Film Fun and Movie Humor

Fruit of the Loom and Fruit of the Earth

Green Leaf and Black Leaf

Helicarb and Heli Coil

Hour after Hour and Shower to Shower

100 Year Nite-lite and Century Night Light

L'air Du Temps and L'air D'or

Long John and Friar John

Marshall Field's and Mrs. Fields

Match and Macho

Mother Bessie's and Mother's Best

Mr. Clean and Master Kleen

Pecan Sandies and Pecan Shortees

Rejuva-nail and Rejuvia

Satin Quick and Suddenly Satin

Silky Touch and Touch O'silk

Subaru and Supra

Surf and Surge

Tic Tac Toe and Tic Tac

T.G.I. Friday's and E.L. Saturday's

Taco Town and Taco Time

Thunderbolt and Thunderbird

Tornado and Typhoon

Vantage and Advance

Wheaties and Oaties

Winterizer and Winterstat

List 1 is the list of marks that do infringe on each other.

SEARCHING TRADEMARKS

Just as individuals may want to perform their own patent searches, some people may want to perform their own trademark searches. There are a variety of ways to get this information. First, searchers can use the PTO Public Search Room. The trademark search library is located on the second floor of the South Tower Building, 2900 Crystal Drive, Arlington, Virginia 22202. Second, searchers may visit a patent and trademark depository library (locations are listed in appendix 1). These libraries have CD-ROMs containing the trademark database of registered and pending marks. Finally, either a private trademark search company or an attorney who deals with trademark law can provide trademark registration information.

Like patents, trademarks are arranged by categories. Fortunately, there are fewer trademark categories than there are patent classifications. There are over four hundred patent classifications, but only about one hundred trademark classifications. One problem may counter this reduction in the number of classifications, however: Searchers looking for a symbol rather than just a trademark name will have to search classification areas for symbols in addition to trademark names.

To search for trademark names, the first step is to identify the proper category for the good or service the trademark represents. Figure 10.1 is a listing of trademark categories. The best way to search for trademark names (not symbols or logos) is to use the CASSIS system. A part of CASSIS (described in chapter 9) is called USAMark. AS with the patent searching techniques of CASSIS, a searcher would enter the proper class number into the system and get a complete listing of all marks in that class. A searcher would then enter the term for the trademark being searched and any matches to that term will be displayed. Because trademark infringement is based not only on exact duplication of an existing mark, but also on any differences in wording that may cause confusion in the mind of the consumer, other words must be searched. Any variant spelling of the mark being sought must also be searched. Any synonym or word that sounds the same but is spelled differently must be searched. Even words in another language must be searched.

As already stated, searching for marks that are words is not as difficult as searching for a patent, but it is difficult enough for an amateur searcher. The real challenge for a trademark searcher lies in the search for symbols and logos (see fig. 10.2).

FIGURE 10.1

U.S. Trademark Classes and Short Titles

001	Raw or Partly Prepared Materials
002	Receptacles
003	Baggage Animal Equipments, Portfolios and Pocketbooks
004	Abrasives and Polishing Materials
005	Adhesives
006	Chemicals and Chemical Compositions
007	Cordage
008	Smokers' Articles, Not Including Tobacco Products
009	Explosives, Firearms, Equipments and Projectiles
010	Fertilizers
011	Inks and Inking Materials
012	Construction Materials
013	Hardware, Plumbing and Steamfitting Supplies
014	Metals, Metal Castings and Forgings
015	Oils and Greases
016	Protective and Decorative Coatings
017	Tobacco Products
018	Medicines and Pharmaceutical Preparations
019	Vehicles
020	Linoleum and Oiled Cloth
021	Electrical Apparatus, Machines and Supplies
022	Games, Toys and Sporting Goods
023	Cutlery, Machinery, Tools and Parts Thereof
024	Laundry Appliances and Machines
025	Locks and Safes
026	Measuring and Scientific Appliances
027	Horological Instruments
028	Jewelry and Precious-metal Ware
029	Brooms, Brushes and Dusters
030	Crockery, Earthenware and Porcelain
031	Filters and Refrigerators
032	Furniture and Upholstery
033	Glassware
034	Heating, Lighting and Ventilating Apparatus
035	Belting, Hose, Machinery Packing and Non-Metallic Tires
036	Musical Instruments and Supplies

037 Paper and Stationery
038 Prints and Publications
039 Clothing
040 Fancy Goods, Furnishings and Notions
041 Canes, Parasols and Umbrellas
042 Knitted, Netted and Textile Fabrics and Substitutes
043 Thread and Yarn
044 Dental, Medical and Surgical Appliances
045 Soft Drinks and Carbonated Waters
046 Foods and Ingredients of Foods
047 Wines
048 Malt Beverages and Liquors
049 Distilled Alcoholic Liquors
050 Merchandise Not Otherwise Classified
051 Cosmetics and Toilet Preparations
052 Detergents and Soaps
100 Miscellaneous
101 Advertising and Business
102 Insurance and Financial
103 Construction and Repair
104 Communication
105 Transportation and Storage
106 Material Treatment
107 Education and Entertainment
200 COLLECTIVE MEMBERSHIP
  A GOODS CERTIFICATION MARK
  B SERVICES CERTIFICATION MARK

Symbols, logos, and graphical representations of a mark are arranged into subcategories within each major category. For example, class 002 Receptacles, has within it a subcategory for graphic marks. The subcategory for a graphic symbol must be located within a given class. If a waste basket manufacturer uses a symbol of a Minuteman in addition to its tradename on its products, the mark will have to be located by first identifying the major category, Receptacles, and then deciding which graphical class the Minuteman falls under. There are hundreds of graphical classes, and each class is

FIGURE 10.2
Registered Trademark

Int. Cl.: 9

Prior U.S. Cls.: 21 and 36

United States Patent and Trademark Office

Reg. No. 1,822,461
Registered Feb. 22, 1994

TRADEMARK
PRINCIPAL REGISTER

PAISLEY PARK ENTERPRISES (MINNESOTA CORPORATION)
7801 AUDUBON ROAD
CHANHASSEN, MN 55317

FOR: SOUND RECORDINGS; NAMELY, PRERECORDED AUDIO CASSETTES, PHONOGRAPH RECORDS AND COMPACT DISCS FEATURING MUSIC AND ENTERTAINMENT; PRE-RECORDED VIDEOTAPES FEATURING MUSIC AND ENTERTAINMENT, IN CLASS 9 (U.S. CLS. 21 AND 36).

FIRST USE 10-13-1992; IN COMMERCE 10-13-1992.

THE MARK COMPRISES A STYLIZED DESIGN OF AN ANKH-LIKE SYMBOL.

SER. NO. 74-375,594, FILED 4-5-1993.

G. T. GLYNN, EXAMINING ATTORNEY

---

further subdivided according to variations in the symbol. The Minuteman will have to be located by first finding the graphic subclass for people. It is class 02, Human Beings.

Within class 02 are further breakdowns of types of human beings. Because this particular human being is a male, the subclass 01 is used. It is the subclass for men. (There is also a subclass for women.) The searcher now has class 02.01. But how can the image be further defined as a Minuteman? There is a further subclass defined as 06—"Men in Colonial dress, Pilgrims, Quakers, and Colonial Minutemen." So a searcher would first have to find the correct categories for the symbol being searched and then search the major category of Receptacles under image class 02.01.06.

Each image identified from USAMark would then need to be retrieved from the CD and evaluated as to its similarity to a mark that was being presented for possible trademark registration—not an easy task because there may be hundreds of marks in a given class/subclass group. The process of searching trademarks is difficult and a complete explanation of it would fill many pages with text and illustrations. The best method for amateur searchers attempting a trademark search is to first familiarize themselves with the products and services available from the PTO at www.uspto.gov and then contact librarians at any PTDL for assistance in searching.

Chapter 11

Questions and Answers about Intellectual Property

It is very difficult for someone who has not worked with the issues of intellectual property to understand the concepts and legal points that apply to it. Specific intellectual property court cases, anecdotes, and incidents that help to clarify individual points are presented throughout this book. A review of the following questions and answers will also help put the concepts into real-world scenarios.

Q. I invent a widget. My brother gives me $1,000 to finance the manufacture of the widgets. So that we can each get 50 percent of the profits on sales of the widgets, can we simply file the patent application in both our names?

A. NO. Patent applications have to be filed in the name of the true inventor(s). If noninventors are named in the application, it can invalidate the patent.

Q. After a reasonable patent search, I file an application for a patent. I find out shortly after mailing my application to the PTO that the invention already exists. Am I liable as an infringer?

A. NO. An application is not an infringement. Only manufacture, sale, or use is infringement.

Q. Are advertising slogans, written statements on T-shirts, or bumper sticker sayings, such as "Where's the Beef," protected by copyright?

A. NO. Copyright is reserved for prose, poetry, maps, artistic works, computer programs, and movies. Advertising slogans are trademarks.

Q. My brother has invented a widget, but is too lazy to patent it. Can he transfer his rights to me and let me patent it?

A. NO. See the answer to the first question.

Q. Does filing a Document Disclosure with the PTO give an inventor a two-year period to file an application without losing the rights to an invention?

A. NO. The only thing a Disclosure will do for you is show evidence of the date of inception of an idea and provide a reliable witness.

Q. Should I not file an application because others can see, copy, or steal my invention by going to the PTO and looking at the filed applications?

A. NO. Applications are filed in secrecy by law. Outsiders have no access to patent applications.

Q. Twenty years ago I invented something but never applied for a patent. I found out that somebody else has recently patented my invention. Do I have any rights to the invention, even if I can prove the date of my invention?

A. NO. The delay in patenting your invention eliminates your rights.

Q. If an invention has been patented by somebody else and the patent has expired, can I get a patent on it myself?

A. NO. You cannot get a patent on anything that has been previously patented. Also, you cannot get a patent on anything shown in a magazine or any other publication anywhere in the world whether it is patented or not. In legal terms, this is called *anticipation.*

Q. If I see an invention that is patented in France, can I get the U.S. patent on it?

A. NO. Only the true inventor has the right to patent in other countries. Also, the publication of a patent in France would come under anticipation laws.

Q. Even though I can't patent the French invention, I decide to go ahead and manufacture it in the United States anyway. Can the French inventor stop me?

A. NO. A patent is enforceable only within the country in which it was issued. The inventor may send Big Pierre to break your thumbs, but legally the inventor can't touch you.

Q. Inventors often send themselves a drawing and description of their invention by certified mail. Is this a good way to protect my rights as an inventor?

A. NO. Certified mail is a poor substitute for a disclosure signed by a witness. Amazingly enough, some patent attorneys still recommend this method of protection for their clients.

Q. Something I have invented appears in the drawings of somebody else's patent, but no mention of it is made in the claims. If I manufacture my own product, am I liable?

A. NO. Only the claims of a patent determine infringement.

Q. Do I have to wait until my patent is granted before I can sell or license my invention to business?

A. NO. Corporate buyers want to purchase inventions as soon as possible after an application is made so that they can get a jump on the competition before an invention is made public.

Q. Does having a patent pending mean that I can sue people who are copying and manufacturing my invention?

A. NO. Patent pending confers no legal rights; however, after the patent is granted, you may sue an infringer.

Q. Do I have to prepare a working model of my invention for submission to the PTO before my patent will be granted?

A. NO. The PTO has not required models for many years.

Q. After seventeen years can a patent be renewed for another seventeen years?

A. NO. It takes an act of Congress to renew a patent. It has never been done.

Q. If a device isn't marked "patented" and doesn't have a patent number, can I copy it?

A. NO. Patents don't have to be marked.

Q. After I have received a patent, can it be declared invalid or taken away from me?

A. YES. It can be declared invalid for many reasons, including overlooked anticipation.

Q. If somebody infringes on my patent, can I file a report with the PTO and will that office take action against the infringer?

A. NO. The PTO is not a law enforcement agency. You alone are responsible for protecting your rights.

Q. If I have an invention that I think would interest a company, can I send a description of it to the firm with an agreement that it will keep the information confidential and pay me if it uses the product?

A. NO. The company will not agree to these terms. It will require you to sign one of its forms stating that the company has no obligation to you, either for payment or to preserve confidentiality.

Q. Words like *kleenex, thermos, radar,* and *sonar* were once trademarks. Are they now generic terms that anyone can use on goods?

A. NO. These terms are still valid trademarks. Xerox went through an extensive campaign several years ago to remind people that Xerox was not a generic term.

Q. Sometimes instead of seeing the standard R in a circle, which designates a registered trademark, you will see a ™. Do the symbols mean the same thing and are they interchangeable?

A. NO. The ™ symbolizes that the term or symbol is being used as a trademark, but is not yet registered.

Q. If I change one or two letters of a trademark in use—for example, changing *xerox* to *xeroks*—can I use the changed term on my goods without infringing on an existing trademark?

A. NO. A trademark has to be unique enough to avoid confusion, mistake, or deception. Usually, changing one or two letters is not enough.

Q. Do I have to have my trademark registered before using it on my goods?

A. NO. A document must be filed with the PTO stating intent to use the mark before it can be registered.

Q. Can copyright be used to protect ideas, systems, or methods of doing things?

A. NO. Copyright can be issued only on a *form* of expression, not the idea per se.

Q. Is a trademark a graphical symbol and a trade name a word?

A. NO. A trademark is any word, symbol, or sound used to identify goods.

Q. Before a copyright is issued does the Copyright Office go through an extensive search, as the PTO does for patents and trademarks?

A. NO. The Copyright Office doesn't care if a work is previously copyrighted or not. If there is an infringement on copyright, it is up to the individual and the courts to straighten things out.

Q. If I make a cassette tape from an album I have at home so that I can play the music in my car, can I be prosecuted for violation of copyright law?

A. YES. Although rarely enforced, this is a violation of copyright.

Q. I invent an electric fork and attempt to trademark it with the name "Electric Fork." Can I do this?

A. NO. A product's common name, even if its function is unique, cannot be protected.

Q. Can sounds be copyrighted?

A. YES. Although very few sounds have been copyrighted, the MGM lion's roar and the NBC chime are two that have been. Recently Harley-Davidson attempted to copyright the sound of its motorcycle engine, claiming the sound was unique and distinctive. As of this writing, the company has not been successful.

Q. If a work does not have a copyright symbol or notice, is it a protected work?

A. YES. A copyright symbol or worded notice has not been required by law since 1988. Assume all material is copyrighted.

Q. What does copyright protect?

A. Copyright, a form of intellectual property law, protects original works of authorship, including literary, dramatic, musical, and artistic works, such as poetry, novels, movies, songs, computer software, and architecture. Copyright does not protect facts, ideas, systems, or methods of operation, although it may protect the way these are expressed.

Q. When is my work protected?

A. Your work is under copyright protection the moment it is created and fixed in a tangible form so that it is perceptible either directly or with the aid of a machine or device.

Q. Why should I register my work if copyright protection is automatic?

A. Registration is recommended for a number of reasons. Many choose to register their works because they wish to have the facts of their copyright on the public record and have a certificate of registration. Registered works may be eligible for statutory damages and attorney's fees in successful litigation. Finally, if registration occurs within five years of publication, it is considered prima facie evidence in a court of law.

Q. Is the Copyright Office the only place to register a copyright?

A. YES. Although copyright application forms are available in public libraries and in some reference books, the U.S. Copyright Office is the only office that can accept applications and issue registrations.

Q. How do I protect my recipe?

A. A mere listing of ingredients is not protected under copyright law. However, when a recipe or formula is accompanied by substantial literary expression in the form of explanations or directions, or when there is a collection of recipes as in a cookbook, there may be a basis for copyright protection.

Q. Who is an author?

A. Under the copyright law, the creator of the original expression in a work is its author. The author is also the owner of the copyright unless there is a written agreement in which the author assigns the copyright to another person or entity, such as a publisher. In cases of works made for hire, the employer or commissioning party is considered to be the author.

Q. How do I copyright a name, title, slogan, or logo?

A. Copyright does not protect names, titles, slogans, or short phrases. In some cases, these things may be protected as trademarks. Contact the U.S. Patent and Trademark Office at (800) 786–9199 for further information. Copyright protection may be available for logo artwork that contains sufficient authorship. In some circumstances, an artistic logo may also be protected as a trademark.

Q. Because virtually everything on the Internet is easily downloaded and copied, anything on the Internet is public domain. Can it be copied without permission?

A. NO. Virtually everything on the Internet is copyrighted and cannot be copied freely and without permission. Being able to copy freely does not constitute legality. A photocopy machine allows one to copy documents with ease, but this does not constitute permission to copy and distribute protected documents.

Q. Is contacting a copyright holder for permission to use copyrighted material always a good idea?

A. NO. The purpose of fair use is to allow copying under certain conditions without permission. One should attempt to contact a copyright holder only after fair use has been ruled out. Otherwise, the copyright system becomes cumbersome and not conducive to advancing knowledge.

Q. May students use pages from government documents without permission for reports and papers?

A. YES. Anybody may use government documents for any purpose without permission. Government documents are not copyrighted.

Q. Do I have to register a work with the Library of Congress in order to claim copyright?

A. NO. Copyright is assumed on creation of the work. Registering the work gives you a better legal framework from which to defend the work against infringes, but it is not necessary.

Q. If I write original stories based on characters in another book, does the new work belong exclusively to me?

A. NO. One of the rights that belong to a copyright holder concerns derivative work. Clearly, basing a story on characters that appear in another copyrighted book is a violation of copyright. The right to use those characters belongs only to the person who created them.

Q. Can copyrighted materials used in multimedia projects remain in a student's portfolio forever?

A. YES. As long as the material is not publicly distributed, the student may archive his or her work.

Q. A school transcribes the lyrics from the album *Grease* and presents it as a minimusical. A student plays the music by ear on the piano, no sheet music is purchased or used, and the students perform every song. There is no admission charge. Is this a violation of copyright?

A. YES. The copyright holder sells the performance rights to any school in a very specific way. It doesn't matter that no sheet music was used or that no admission was charged or that this is an educational use. The school has to buy the performance rights.

Q. A health teacher tapes an *I Love Lucy* episode on personal hygiene to show the following week in class. The local television station that broadcast the program denies permission when asked and states this is a violation of copyright law. Can the station deny this permission?

A. NO. The television station can neither deny or grant permission. It doesn't hold the copyright on *I Love Lucy*. However, the teacher still cannot show the episode. A public display of the entire program is a violation of copyright.

Q. How long does the registration process take and when will I get my copyright certificate?

A. The time the Copyright Office requires to process an application varies, depending on the amount of material the office is receiving. You may expect a certificate of registration within approximately eight months of submission.

Q. How can I obtain copies of someone else's work and/or registration certificate?

A. The Copyright Office will not honor a request for a copy of someone else's work without written authorization from the copyright owner or from his or her designated agent if that work is still under copyright protection, unless the work is involved in litigation. Written permission from the copyright owner or a litigation statement is required before copies can be made available. A certificate of registration for any registered work can be obtained for a fee of $25. Circular 6 provides additional information.

Q. Can I obtain a list of songs or movies in the public domain from the Copyright Office?

A. NO. The Copyright Office neither compiles nor maintains such a list. A search of the office's records, however, may reveal whether a particular work has fallen into the public domain. The Copyright Office will conduct a search of its records by the title of a work, an author's name, or a claimant's name. You may pay a per-hour search fee, or you may search the records in person without paying a fee.

Q. What is mandatory deposit?

A. Copies of all works under copyright protection that have been published in the United States are required to be deposited with the Copyright Office within three months of the date of first publication.

Q. Do I have to register with the Copyright Office to be protected?

A. NO. In general, registration is voluntary. Copyright exists from the moment the work is created. You will have to register, however, if you wish to bring a lawsuit for infringement of a U.S. work.

Q. How do I register my copyright?

A. To register a work, you need to submit a completed application form, a nonrefundable filing fee, and a nonreturnable copy or copies of the work to be registered.

Q. Can I make copies of the application form?

A. YES. You can make copies of copyright forms if they meet the following criteria: photocopied back-to-back and head-to-head on a single sheet of 8 1/2-by-11-inch white paper. In other words, your copy must look just like the original.

Q. What is a deposit?

A. A deposit is usually one copy (if unpublished) or two copies (if published) of the work to be registered for copyright. In certain cases, such as works of the visual arts, identifying material such as a photograph may be used instead. The deposit is sent with the application and fee and becomes the property of the Library of Congress.

Q. Do I have to send in my work?

A. YES. You must send the required copy or copies of the work to be registered. These copies will not be returned. Upon their deposit in the Copyright Office, under sections 407 and 408 of the Copyright law, all copies, phono records, and identifying material, including those deposited in connection with claims that have been refused registration, are the property of the United States government.

Q. May I register more than one work on the same application? Where do I list the titles?

A. You may register unpublished works as a collection on one application with one title for the entire collection if certain conditions are met. It is not necessary to list the individual titles in your collection, although you may do so by completing a Continuation Sheet. Published works may only be registered as a collection if they were actually first published as a collection and if other requirements have been met.

Q. What is the difference between form PA and form SR?

A. These forms are for registering two different types of copyrightable subject matter that may be embodied in a recording. Form PA is used for the registration of music and/or lyrics (as well as other works of the performing arts), even if your song is on a cassette. Form SR is used for registering the performance and production of a particular recording of sounds.

Q. Do I have to renew my copyright?

A. NO. Works created on or after January 1, 1978, are not subject to renewal registration. As to works published or registered before January 1, 1978, renewal registration is optional after twenty-eight years but does provide certain legal advantages.

Q. Can I submit my manuscript on a computer disk?

A. NO. There are many different software formats and the Copyright Office does not have the equipment to accommodate all of them. Therefore, the Copyright Office still generally requires a printed copy or audio recording of the work for deposit.

Q. Can I submit a CD-ROM of my work?

A. YES. The deposit requirement consists of the best edition of the CD-ROM package of any work, including the accompanying operating software, instruction manual, and a printed version, if included in the package.

Q. Does copyright now protect architecture?

A. YES. Architectural works became subject to copyright protection on December 1, 1990. The copyright law defines *architectural work* as "the design of a building embodied in any tangible medium of expression, including a building, architectural plans, or drawings." Copyright protection extends to any architectural work created on or after December 1, 1990, and any architectural work that on December 1, 1990, was not constructed and was embodied in unpublished plans or drawings. Architectural works embodied in buildings constructed before December 1, 1990, are not eligible for copyright protection.

Q. Can I register a diary I found in my grandmother's attic?

A. You can register copyright in the diary only if you are the transferee (by will, by inheritance). Copyright is the right of the author of the work or the author's heirs or assignees, not of the one who only owns or possesses the physical work itself.

Q. Can foreigners register their works in the United States?

A. YES. Any work that is protected by U.S. copyright law can be registered. This includes many works of foreign origin. All works that are unpublished, regardless of the nationality of the author, are protected in the United States. Works that are first published in the United States or in a country with which we have a copyright treaty or that are created by a citizen or domiciliary of a country with which we have a copyright treaty are also protected and may therefore be registered with the U.S. Copyright Office.

Q. What is a work made for hire?

A. Although the general rule is that the person who creates the work is its author, there is an exception to that principle. A work made for hire is a work prepared by an employee within the scope of his or her employment or a work specially ordered or commissioned in certain specified circumstances. When a work qualifies as a work made for hire, the employer or commissioning party is considered to be the author.

Q. Can a minor claim copyright?

A. YES. Minors may claim copyright, and the Copyright Office does issue registrations to minors, but state laws may regulate the business dealings involving copyrights owned by minors. For information on relevant state laws, consult an attorney.

Q. Do I have to use my real name on the form? Can I use a stage name or a pen name?

A. There is no legal requirement that the author be identified by his or her real name on the application form. If filing under a fictitious name, check the "Pseudonymous" box at space 2.

Q. What is publication?

A. Publication has a technical meaning in copyright law. According to the statute, "Publication is the distribution of copies or phono records of a work to the public by sale or other transfer of ownership, or by rental, lease, or lending. The offering to distribute copies or phono records to a group of persons for purposes of further distribution, public performance, or public display constitutes publication. A public performance or display of a work does not of itself constitute publication." Generally, publication occurs on the date on which copies of the work are first made available to the public.

Q. Does my work have to be published to be protected?

A. NO. Publication is not necessary for copyright protection.

Q. Are copyrights transferable?

A. YES. Like any other property, the owner may transfer all or part of the rights in a work to another.

Q. Can I copyright the name of my band?

A. NO. Copyright law does not protect names. Some names may be protected under trademark law. Contact the U.S. Patent and Trademark Office for further information.

Q. How do I protect my idea?

A. Copyright does not protect ideas, concepts, systems, or methods of doing something. You may express your ideas in writing or drawings and claim copyright in your description, but be aware that copyright will not protect the idea itself as revealed in your written or artistic work.

Q. How long does copyright last?

A. The Sonny Bono Copyright Term Extension Act, signed into law on October 27, 1998, amends the provisions concerning duration of copyright protection. The terms of copyright are generally extended for an additional twenty years. Specific provisions are summarized in figure 3.2 in chapter 3.

Q. How much do I have to change in my own work to make a new claim of copyright?

A. You may make a new claim in your work if the changes are substantial and creative—something more than just editorial changes or minor changes. This would qualify as a new derivative work. For instance, simply making spelling corrections throughout a work does not warrant a new registration; adding an additional chapter would.

Q. How do I get my work into the Library of Congress?

A. Copies of works deposited for copyright registration or in fulfillment of the mandatory deposit requirement are available to the Library of Congress for its collections. The library reserves the right to select or reject any published work for its permanent collections based on the research needs of Congress, the nation's scholars, and the nation's libraries. If you would like further information on the library's selection policies, you may contact: Library of Congress, Collections Policy Office, 101 Independence Avenue, S.E., Washington, DC 20540.

Q. What is a copyright notice? How do I put a copyright notice on my work?

A. A copyright notice is an identifier placed on copies of the work to inform the world of copyright ownership. Although use of a copyright notice was once required as a condition of copyright protection, it is now optional. Use of the notice is the responsibility of the copyright owner and does not require advance permission from, or registration with, the Copyright Office.

Q. How do I collect royalties?

A. The collection of royalties is usually a matter of private arrangements between an author and publisher or other users of the author's work. The Copyright Office plays no role in the execution of contractual terms or business practices. There are copyright licensing organizations and publications rights clearinghouses that distribute royalties for their members.

Q. Somebody infringed my copyright. What can I do?

A. A party may seek to protect his or her copyrights against unauthorized use by filing a civil lawsuit in federal district court. If you believe that your copyright has been infringed, consult an attorney. In cases of willful infringement for profit, the U.S. Attorney may initiate a criminal investigation.

Q. Is my copyright good in other countries?

A. The United States has copyright relations with more than one hundred countries throughout the world, and as a result of these agreements, we honor each other's citizens' copyrights. However, the United States does not have such copyright relationships with every country.

Q. How do I protect my sighting of Elvis?

A. Copyright law does not protect sightings. However, copyright law will protect your photo (or other depiction) of your sighting of Elvis. Just send it to the Copyright Office with a form VA application and the filing fee. No one can lawfully use your photo of your sighting, although someone else may file his or her own photo of a sighting. Copyright law protects the original photograph, not the subject of the photograph.

Q. How do I get permission to use somebody else's work?

A. You can ask for it. If you know who the copyright owner is, you may contact the owner directly. If you are not certain about the ownership or have other related questions, you may wish to request the Copyright Office to conduct a search of its records for a per-hour fee.

Q. Could I be sued for using somebody else's work? How about quotes or samples?

A. If you use a copyrighted work without authorization, the owner may be entitled to bring an infringement action against you. In certain circumstances under the fair use doctrine, a quote or a sample may be used without permission. However, in cases of doubt, the Copyright Office recommends that permission be obtained.

Questions on Fair Use

Q. A library stores bibliographic instruction materials on a local password-protected site. The materials are used in distance learning. If the library puts these materials on the Web and makes them freely available, would the library be liable if some of the materials are in violation of copyright?

A. The library would be liable if the library was the ISP and if the library had knowledge of the materials being in violation of copyright. Normally, university libraries are not ISPs. The university is. Normally public libraries are not ISPs. The city or municipality is. Knowledge of a violation of copyright is a primary concept in the DMCA.

Q. To be safe should libraries request written permission for all copyrighted materials that reside on a library's website?

A. This defeats the whole concept of fair use. The act of requesting permission is time-consuming and labor-intensive, and requires the retention of many records. The better procedure is to first rule out fair use.

Q. Since the DMCA was passed in 1998, is the 1978 copyright law no longer valid?

A. The DMCA is an amendment to the 1978 Copyright Law and is not a new law. The 1978 Copyright Law is still valid.

Q. Fair use allows libraries to place on reserve copyrighted materials for "one-time" use if they are used for educational purposes. At a university or college, what is "one time"—one semester? one year? one class period?

A. One-time use in a university library setting is one semester whether that one semester is ten weeks or fifteen weeks. However, this "one time" explanation does not apply to distance education courses. In distance education situations, like so much in fair use, it is not clear. The law does not spell out what one-time use means for distance education.

Q. If an electronic text used for distance education has integrated software that prohibits downloading more than a few paragraphs of the text, can an instructor use a software package that allows students to copy more than that?

A. It depends. As with a lot of texts, full-text articles, or other products that an educational institution loads on its online systems, permission to use these materials and the restrictions on them are spelled out in the contract with the vendor who supplies the product. Copyright law and fair use concepts are not valid in this type of situation. Users should read and be familiar with the *contract* to determine what copying is allowed. In situations where contracts are not involved, it should be noted that the DMCA has restrictions on using technical methods to bypass anti-copying devices built into the software.

Q. In interlibrary loan situations, it is permissible in accordance with fair use to send a copy of an article held by a library to a user associated with another library, as long as the use is for educational purposes. If an article exists electronically and is sent electronically—e.g., by Ariel—is this permissible in accordance with fair use?

A. Once again, as with so much in fair use, it depends. And once again, the answer lies not with the concepts of fair use, but with the contract with the vendor of the product you are transmitting electronically. Some allow such electronic transmission; some do not. The fear of vendors is that once the article is transmitted in a digital form, it is available for free distribution across the Internet. This distribution is not as simple with a paper copy. Interestingly, even if a vendor does not allow electronic distribution of a digitized article, if an article is printed out and a *paper* copy of the digitized article sent through interlibrary loan, this is permissible by fair use.

Q. If a library is using e-reserves—that is, reserve material residing on a website—can the library make the reserve material available for distance education?

A. It depends. Check the contract with the vendor who supplies the material. In most cases where the library digitizes paper material then makes it available for distance education, access to the reserve material would have to be limited to those enrolled in the class that relates to the material. This is a touchy area, because some publishers do not allow digitizing of their paper products for such uses for fear that students enrolled in the class would have the ability to download the material and distribute it. In this situation, a library would have to check with the publisher to confirm proper use of the material in an electronic format. The Copyright Clearance Center (www.copyright.com) is a good place to pursue these clearances. Some libraries attach a note to the serial record that informs potential users of what permissions the publisher is willing to grant, such as "allows photocopying" or "allows e-transfers."

Q. Can an instructor show a copy of a video in class if the library owns the original?

A. NO. Such use is permitted only if the copy is a replacement for a damaged video that the library owns. Section 108 of the Copyright Law spells out the lawful uses of videos in educational settings. In Section 110(1), an exemption is made for a "public performance" of a video in a classroom situation. However, this exemption does not apply to videos shown over the Internet as part of distance education courses.

Q. Can students place their class notes from an instructor's lecture on a website for other students to copy?

A. NO. The class notes are clearly a derivative work from fixed notes that an instructor uses for the lecture. Rights to derivative works are included in the five rights given to copyright holders.

Q. Many websites run into many pages. If a library's multipaged website contains registered copyright material, does each page of the website have to carry a copyright symbol or notice?

A. Since 1988, copyright symbols or notices do not have to accompany copyrighted material. In 1988, the United States joined the Berne Convention, which is a treaty between virtually all industrialized nations to accept each other's copyright laws and to establish some worldwide consistency to copyright laws. Because most nations do not use copyright symbols, none of the members of the Berne Convention is required to have copyright holders identify their materials.

Q. A faculty member scans copyrighted articles from a journal and puts them on a server not associated with a university. She makes access to the articles protected by a password and limits access to those in her class. Is this copyright infringement?

A. No court case has yet defined this aspect of copyright law. On the surface, the faculty member is taking every precaution to assure that the scanned articles are being used in accordance with fair use. However, if a student downloads one of the articles and distributes it to others outside the class, this would be infringement. In a worst case scenario, the owner of the scanned articles could, under DMCA guidelines, contact the university and ask that the articles be removed immediately. Liability in this case would be unclear, because the university is an ISP and could claim exemption from prosecution.

Q. Is it permissible to use copyrighted material if there is no charge for the final work the copyrighted material is used in?

A. Not always. One of the four guidelines for fair use is that the copyrighted material used does not detrimentally affect the value of the copyrighted material, but this is not the only guideline. Other factors may make this practice illegal even if it is for a nonprofit use.

Q. Is using a short excerpt from a book for scholarly use considered fair use?

A. Not always. A short excerpt from a children's book may actually constitute a significant portion of that book and would not be allowed under fair use guidelines. The important issue is the percentage of the entire work the excerpt constitutes, not the size of the excerpt itself.

Q. A teacher videotaped the ABC news report showing Bill Clinton leaving the White House. She made the tape at home on her VCR. She uses the entire program every year in her classroom. Is this fair use?

A. NO. Publicly broadcast news events can only be shown for ten days afterward unless the copyright holder grants greater allowances for educators.

Q. The owner of the local video store donates one videotape rental-free to the school every Friday. The video is shown in a classroom to reward students with perfect attendance. Is this fair use?

A. NO. Reward is explicitly excluded under copyright guidelines. To show a movie for entertainment purposes, you must obtain a version from an authorized distributor who can license you to show it.

Q. A teacher rents *Gone with the Wind* to show the burning of Atlanta scene to her class during their study of the Civil War. Is this fair use?

A. YES. This is a clear example of fair use.

Q. A school purchases one copy of a typing tutorial program at keeps it in the library. The program is checked out to individual students to take home for a week and load onto their home computers. The students are required to erase the program at the end of the two weeks. Is this fair use?

A. YES. The school must make serious efforts, however, to make sure that the program is erased from the students' home computers.

Q. A student doing a report discovers how to copy several frames of the Zapruder film of the Kennedy assassination from a CD-ROM encyclopedia. He presents the report to his classmates, then posts it on the school LAN. Is this fair use?

A. YES. Two important items make this fair use. First, the clip is short and second, it is being used for educational purposes. It is also important that the school LAN not be accessible to the outside world.

Q. A student finds a photo online dramatizing a Viking landing in America. Because the school symbol is a Viking, she uses this photo on the school's web page, giving credit to the site from which it was copied. Is this fair use?

A. NO. Internet pages are copyrighted automatically. The student cannot post anything for the general public without permission even if credit is given. Use in a class report, however, would be fair use.

Q. A student doing a multimedia art project uses copyrighted images of Frank Lloyd Wright buildings downloaded from the Web. She submits this project to a competition for classroom multimedia projects. Is this covered under fair use?

A. YES. As long as the competition is expressly for classroom work by students, the use is permitted. If the resulting projects were distributed on CD-ROM or posted on a Website, this would not be fair use.

Q. An instructional services employee at a high school tapes "The CBS News" every day in case teachers need it. Is this fair use?

A. NO. Schools may not tape in anticipation of requests. They can act only on actual requests.

Q. A high school video class produces a student video that is sold at community events to raise money for video equipment for the school. The students use well-known popular music clips in the video. The money all goes to the school and the songs are fully listed in the credits. Is this fair use?

A. NO. This is not instructional or educational use. The fact that money is being charged is irrelevant. The infringement lies in the use of copyrighted materials for noninstructional purposes.

Appendix A

Patent and Trademark Depository Libraries Program

A patent and trademark depository library (PTDL) is a library designated by the U.S. Patent and Trademark Office (PTO) to receive and house copies of U.S. patents and patent and trademark materials, to make them freely available to the public, and to actively disseminate patent and trademark information.

The Patent and Trademark Depository Library Program began in 1871 when federal law first provided for the distribution of printed patents to libraries for use by the public. During the program's early years, twenty-two libraries, mostly public and all but several located east of the Mississippi River, elected to participate. Since 1977, the PTDL network has grown to four times its original size. Currently, about half the membership is academic libraries with nearly as many public libraries.

Many states value the presence of a PTDL because it is a rich local resource for small businesses, research and development firms, university and governmental laboratories, and amateur inventors. Access to trademark information is in high demand by local businesses.

Each PTDL must pay a nominal annual statutory fee to the U.S. Patent and Trademark Office. In return, the following materials are provided to assist the amateur searcher: Utility, Design, Plant, and Reissue Patents; *The Official Gazette of the United States Patent and Trademark Office* (both patent and trademark sections); and all PTO search tools, indices, and directories. The following list of PTDLs includes contact information.

Abigail S. Timme Library
Ferris State University
1010 Campus Drive
Big Rapids, MI 49307-2279
231-591-3500

Ablah Library
Wichita State University
1845 Fairmount
Wichita, KS 67260
316-978-3155

Akron-Summit County Public
  Library
1040 E. Tallmadge Avenue
Akron, OH 44310
330-643-9000

Anchorage Municipal Libraries
Z. J. Loussac Public Library
3600 Denali Street
Anchorage, AK 99503-6093
907-562-7323

Arkansas State Library
P.O. Box 2040
State University, AR 72467
870-972-3077

Auburn University Libraries
231 Mell Street
Auburn University, AL 36849-
  5606
334-844-1738

Bailey/Howe Library
University of Vermont
Burlington, VT 05405
802-656-2542

Birmingham Public Library
2100 Park Place
Birmingham, AL 35203-2974
205-226-3610

Boston Public Library
P.O. Box 286
Boston, MA 02117
617-536-5400

Broward County Main Library
100 S. Andrews Ave.
Fort Lauderdale, FL 33301
954-357-7444

Buffalo and Erie County Public
  Library
Lafayette Square
Buffalo, NY 14203
716-858-7101

California State Library
Library-Courts Building
P.O. Box 942837
Sacramento, CA 94287
916-653-6033

The Carnegie Library of
  Pittsburgh
4400 Forbes Avenue
Pittsburgh, PA 15213
412-622-3138

Centennial Science and
  Engineering Library
The University of New Mexico
Albuquerque, NM 87131-1466
505-277-4412

Central Library of Rochester
  and Monroe County
115 South Avenue
Rochester, NY 14604
716-428-7300

Chester Fritz Library
  University of North Dakota
University Avenue and
  Centennial Dr.
P.O. Box 9000
Grand Forks, ND 58202
701-777-4888

Chicago Public Library
400 South State Street
Chicago, IL 60605
312-747-4450

Clark County Library
1401 E. Flamingo Road
Las Vegas, NV 89119
702-733-7810

Cleveland Public Library
325 Superior Avenue, N. E.
Cleveland, OH 44114-1271
216-623-2800

D. H. Hill Library
North Carolina State University
2205 Hillsborough Street
Box 7111
Raleigh, NC 27695-7111
919-515-2935

Denver Public Library
10 W. Fourteenth Ave. Pkwy.
Denver, CO 80204
303-691-0458

Engineering and Physical Sciences
Library
University of Maryland
College Park, MD 20742
301-405-9157

Engineering Library
University of Nebraska-Lincoln
Nebraska Hall, Room W203
2nd Floor West
City Campus 0516
Lincoln, NE 68588-4100
402-472-3411

Evansdale Library
West Virginia University
P.O. Box 6105
Morgantown, WV 26506-6105
304-293-4695 ext. 5113

Fondren Library
Rice University
P.O. Box 1892
Houston, TX 77251-1892
713-348-5483

Founders Library
Howard University
500 Howard Place, NW
Washington, DC 20059
202-806-7234

The Free Library of Philadelphia
1901 Vine Street
Philadelphia, PA 19103
215-686-5322

General Library
University of Puerto Rico at
Mayagüez
P.O. Box 9022
Mayagüez, Puerto Rico 00681-9022
787-832-4040 ext. 2022

Georgia Institute of Technology
Price Gilbert Memorial Library
Atlanta, GA 30332-0900
404-894-4508

Government Information Center
1515 Young Street, 6th Floor
Dallas, TX 75201
214-670-1468

Great Lakes Patent and Trademark
Center
Detroit Public Library
5201 Woodward Avenue
Detroit, MI 48202
313-833-3379 or 800-547-0619

Hartford Public Library
500 Main Street
Hartford, CT 06103
860-543-8628

Hawaii State Library
Second Floor
478 S. King Street
Honolulu, HI 96813-2994
808-586-3477

Illinois State Library
300 S. Second Street
Springfield, IL 62701-1976
217-782-7596

Indianapolis-Marion County
 Public Library
P.O. Box 211
Indianapolis, IN 46206
317-269-1700

James Branch Cabell Library
Virginia Commonwealth
 University
901 Park Avenue
 P.O. Box 842033
Richmond, VA 23284-2033
804-828-1104

Kurt F. Wendt Library
University of Wisconsin-Madison
215 N. Randall Avenue
Madison, WI 53706-1688
608-262-6845

Library of Science and Medicine
Rutgers, The State University of
 New Jersey
165 Bevier Road
Piscataway, NJ 08854-8009
732-445-3850

Linda Hall Library
St. Louis Public Library
5109 Cherry Street
Kansas City, MO 64110-2498
816-363-4600 or 800-662-1545

Los Angeles Public Library
Downtown Los Angeles
630 W. Fifth Street
Los Angeles, CA 90071
213-228-7000

Louisville Free Public Library
301 York Street
Louisville, KY 40203
502-574-1611

Media Union Library
University of Michigan
Ann Arbor, MI 48109-2136
313-764-5298

Melville Library
Room 1101
SUNY at Stony Brook
Stony Brook, NY 11794
631-632-7148

Memphis/Shelby County Public
 Library and Information Center
1850 Peabody Ave.
Memphis, TN 38104
901-725-8877

Miami-Dade Public Library
101 W. Flagler Street
Miami, FL 33130
305-375-2665

Milwaukee Public Library
814 W. Wisconsin Avenue
Milwaukee, WI 53233
414-286-3151

Minneapolis Public Library
300 Nicollet Mall
Minneapolis, MN 55401-1992
612-630-6120

Mississippi Library Commission
1221 Ellis Avenue
Jackson, MS 39209
877-594-5733 (toll free) or
    601-961-4120

Montana Tech Library
University of Montana
Butte, MT 59701
406-496-4281

New Hampshire State Library
20 Park Street
Concord, NH 03301
603-271-2143

New Haven Free Public Library
133 Elm Street
New Haven, CT 06510
203-946-8130

New York State Library
Cultural Education Center
Albany, NY 12230
518-474-5355

Newark Public Library
3rd Floor, Main Library
5 Washington Street
Newark, NJ 07101
973-733-7779

Noble Science and Engineering
    Library
Arizona State University
P.O. Box 871006
Tempe, AZ 85287-1006
480-965-6164

Ohio State University Library
1858 Neil Avenue Mall
Columbus, OH 43210
614-292-6154

Oklahoma State University
    Library
Stillwater, OK 74078-1071
405-744-0729 or
    877-744-9161 (toll free)

Paul L. Boley Law Library
Northwestern School of Law of
    Lewis and Clark College
10015 SW Terwilliger Blvd.
Portland, OR 97219
503-768-6786

Penn State University
Paterno Library
Business Library
University Park, PA 16802
814-865-6369

Physical Sciences and Engineering
    Library
University of Massachusetts
Amherst, MA 01003
413-545-1370

Providence Public Library
225 Washington Street
Providence, RI 02903
401-455-8027

The Public Library of Cincinnati
800 Vine Street
Cincinnati, OH 45202-2071
513-369-6971

R. M. Cooper Library
Clemson University Library
Box 343001
Clemson, SC 29634-3001
864-656-3024

Raymond H. Fogler Library
University of Maine
Orono, ME 04469-5729
207-581-1678

St. Louis Public Library
Central Library
1301 Olive Street
St. Louis, MO 63103
314-241-2288

San Antonio Public Library
600 Soledad
San Antonio, TX 78205
210-207-2500

San Diego Public Library
1105 Front Street
San Diego, CA 92101-3904
619-531-3900

San Francisco Public Library
100 Larkin Street (at Grove)
San Francisco, CA 94102
415-557-4400

Science, Industry and
    Business Library
New York Public Library
188 Madison Avenue (at 34th
    Street)
New York, NY 10016
212 592-7000

Siegesmund Engineering Library
Purdue University
1530 Steward Center
West Lafayette, IN 47907
765-494-2800

South Dakota School of Mines
    and Technology
Devereaux Library
501 East St. Joseph Street
Rapid City, SD 57701-3995
605-394-1275

State Library of Iowa
1112 East Grand Avenue
Des Moines, IA 50319
515-281-4105

Sterling C. Evans Library
Texas A&M University
College Station, TX 77843-5000
979-845-5745

Stevenson Science and
    Engineering Library
Vanderbilt University
419 21st Avenue South
Nashville, TN 37240
615-322-2717

Sunnyvale Center for Innovation,
    Invention and Ideas
465 S. Mathilda Ave.
Suite 300
Sunnyvale, CA 94086
408-730-7290

Tampa Campus Library
University of South Florida
4202 E. Fowler Avenue
LIB 122
Tampa, FL 33620-5400
813-974-2726

Texas Tech University Libraries
18th and Boston
P.O. Box 40002
Lubbock, TX 79409-0002
806-742-2282

Troy H. Middleton Library
Louisiana State University
53 Middleton Library
Baton Rouge, LA 70803
225-388-8875

The University Libraries
1664 N. Virginia St.
Reno, NV 89557
775-784-6500, ext. 257

University of Central Florida
  Libraries
P.O. Box 162666
Orlando, FL 32816
407-823-2562

University of Delaware Library
181 South College Avenue
Newark, DE 19717-5267
302-831-2965

University of Idaho Library
Moscow, ID 83844-2350
208-885-6584

The University of Texas at Austin
McKinney Engineering Library
ECJ 1.300
Austin, Texas 78713
512-495-4500

University of Utah Marriott
  Library
295 S 1500 E, Level 1
Salt Lake City, UT 84112-0860
801-581-8558

University of Washington
Engineering Library
Box 352170
Seattle, WA 98195-2170
206-543-0740

Wright State University Library
Paul Laurence Dunbar Library
Dayton, OH 45435
937-775-2380

Wyoming State Library
2301 Capitol Ave.
Cheyenne, WY 82002-0060
307-777-6333

Appendix B

Intellectual Properties Websites

BitLaw
  http://www.bitlaw.com/

Center for Intellectual Property and Copyright in the Digital
  Environment http://www.umuc.edu/distance/cip/

Conference on Collective Strategies in Approaching Copyright Issues
  Affecting CIC and Regent Institutions
  http://www.cic.uiuc.edu/resources/ip/iowarpt.html

Copyright and Distance Education
  http://www.uidaho.edu/evo/dist12.html

Copyright and Distance Education Resources
  http://www.indiana.edu/~icy/copyright.html

Copyright and Fair Use, Stanford University
  http://fairuse.stanford.edu/

Copyright & You—a Symposium on Intellectual Property in
  the Electronic Age
  http://www.libraries.psu.edu/iasweb/copyrt/copyrt.htm

Copyright and the Internet
  http://mason.gmu.edu/~montecin/copyright-internet.htm

Copyright Basics—Division of Instructional Improvement and
  Instructional Technology
  http://www.doiiit.gmu.edu/copyright.htm

Copyright Clearance Center, Inc.
http://www.copyright.com/

Copyright Compliance Connection
http://www.goehner.com/piracy.htm

Copyright Considerations in Distance Education and Technology-
Mediated Instruction
http://www.aacc.nche.edu/headline/070700head1.htm

Copyright, Fair Use and Licensing in a Digital World
http://www-ninch.cni.org/ISSUES/COPYRIGHT.html

Copyright in the Digital Environment
http://www.cnn.com/LAW/trials.and.cases/case.files/0008/copyright/
linkframeset.exclude.html

Copyright in the Library
http://www.utsystem.edu/OGC/IntellectualProperty/l-intro.htm

Copyright in the Library—Fair Use: Reserve Room Operations, Print
Copies
http://www.utsystem.edu/OGC/IntellectualProperty/l-respri.htm

Copyright Issues
http://mason.gmu.edu/~montecin/cpyrght.htm

Copyright Law in the Electronic Environment
http://www.utsystem.edu/OGC/IntellectualProperty/faculty.htm

Copyright Law of the United States of America and Related Laws
Contained in Title 17 of the United States Code
http://www.loc.gov/copyright/title17/

Copyright Management Center
http://www.iupui.edu/~copyinfo/

Copyright on the Internet
http://www.fplc.edu/tfield/copynet.htm

Copyright Resources on the Internet
http://groton.k12.ct.us/mts/pt2a.htm

Copyright Website
http://www.benedict.com/

Crash Course in Copyright
http://www.utsystem.edu/OGC/IntellectualProperty/cprtindx.htm

Cyber Law (TM)—Famous Trademarks
http://www.cyberlaw.com/cylw0296.html

Cyberlaw Periodical
http://www.cyberlaw.com

Cyber Property, Citation, and the World Wide Web
http://www.cas.usf.edu/english/walker/papers/cyberprop.html

Cyberspace Law Center
http://www.cybersquirrel.com/clc/clcindex.html

Cyberspace Law for Non-Lawyers
http://www.counsel.com/cyberspac/copyright.html

Digital Object Identifier System
http://www.doi.org/

Distance Learning and Copyright from Copyright Management Center
http://www.iupui.edu/~copyinfo/disted.html

Fair Use of Copyrighted Works, a Crucial Element in Educating America
http://www.cetus.org/fairindex.html

General Information about Copyright
http://www.patents.com/copyrigh.htm

How to Investigate the Copyright Status of a Work
http://www.loc.gov/copyright/circs/circ22.html

iCopyright.com—Instant Clearance Service
http://icopyright.com/

Intellectual Property in the Information Age: A Classroom Guide to
Copyright
http://www.cas.usf.edu/english/walker/papers/copyright/ipdummie.
html

Intellectual Property Magazine
www.ipmag.com

Intellectual Property Mall Pointer Page
http://www.fplc.edu/ipmall/pointbox.htm

Kuester Law Technology Law Resource
http://www.kuesterlaw.com

Navigating Copyright in Cyberspace
http://mason.gmu.edu/~montecin/copyright-internet/index.htm

"No Cense"—Copyright Reform Campaign (archive)
http://www.mindspring.com/~mccarthys/no-cense/

Penn State University Libraries—Copyright Resources
   http://www.libraries.psu.edu/crsweb/select/manual/copyright.htm

Primer on the Digital Millennium
   http://www.arl.org/info/frn/copy/primer.html

Stanford University Fair Use Site
   http://fairuse.stanford.edu/

Study on Distance Education and Digital Technologies
   http://www.arl.org/info/frn/copy/disted.html

Tech.Learning—The Educators' Lean and Mean No FATGuide to Fair
   Use by Hall Davidson
   http://www.techlearning.com/content/speak/articles/copyright.html

Texas Intellectual Property Presentations
   http://www.utsystem.edu/OGC/IntellectualProperty/present.htm

Texas System Copyright Management Center
   http://www.utsystem.edu/OGC/IntellectualProperty/cprtindx.htm

Trademark Information
   http://www.naming.com/trademark2.html

United States Copyright Office
   http://lcweb.loc.gov/copyright/

United States Patent and Trademark Office Home Page
   http://www.uspto.gov/

US Code Home—Title 17—Copyrights
   http://www.access.gpo.gov/uscode/title17/title17.html

U.S. Copyright Office Forms
   http://www.loc.gov/copyright/forms/

A Visit to Copyright Bay
   http://www.stfrancis.edu/cid/copyrightbay/

Wacky Patents
   http://inventors.about.com/cs/wackypatents/index.htm?once=true&

When Works Pass into the Public Domain
   http://www.unc.edu/~unclng/public-d.htm

World Intellectual Property Organization (WIPO)
   http://www.wipo.int/

Yale University Copyright Reference
http://www.library.yale.edu:80/~okerson/copyrproj.html

Index

Page numbers in italics refer to figures and illustrations.

Timothy Lee Wherry is on the faculty at Pennsylvania State University and is the director at the Robert E. Eiche Library. Formerly he was Director of Learning Resources and Assistant Dean of Information Services. Wherry's research interests are in intellectual property, particularly as it applies to the Internet. He has written numerous articles on intellectual property as well as a book, *Patent Searching for Librarians and Inventors* (ALA 1995). In 1994 he received the Penn State Altoona Grace D. Long Faculty Excellence Award.

WITHDRAWAL